THE UPCYCLED T-SHIRT

28 Easy-to-Make Projects That Save the Planet

Clothing, Accessories, Home Decor & Gifts

Jenelle Montilone

stashBOOKS®

an imprint of C&T Publishing

Publisher: Amy Marson

Creative Director: Gailen Runge

Art Director: Kristy Zacharias

Editor: S. Michele Fry

Technical Editors: Julie Waldman and Mary E. Flynn

Cover/Book Designer: April Mostek

Production Coordinators: Zinnia Heinzmann and Rue Flaherty

Production Editor: Katie Van Amburg

Illustrator: Lon Eric Craven

Photo Stylist: Lauren Toker

Photo Assistant: Mary Peyton Peppo

Style photography by Nissa Brehmer and instructional photography by Diane Pedersen, unless otherwise noted

Published by Stash Books, an imprint of C&T Publishing, Inc., P.O. Box 1456, Lafayette, CA 94549

Library of Congress Cataloging-in-Publication Data

Montilone, Jenelle, 1984- author.

The upcycled T-shirt : 28 easy-to-make projects that save the planet - clothing, accessories, home decor & gifts / Jenelle Montilone.

 pages cm

ISBN 978-1-60705-971-4 (soft cover)

1. T-shirts--Recycling. I. Title.

TT675.M66 2015

687--dc23

2014033385

Printed in China

10 9 8 7 6 5 4 3 2 1

Dedication

My dedication is to those who have come before—may I be a worthy heir. To those who will come after—may I be a worthy ancestor. For those I walk alongside—may I be a worthy companion. To a legacy of courage, hope, honor, and love—I wrote this book for you.

Acknowledgments

If not for those of you who believed in me, even when I didn't believe in myself, my words would have never found their way to these pages. I'm grateful for the unconditional love and support of my family and friends. Nothing you do goes unnoticed.

To Grammy and Nana for all the love.

A special thank-you to Lorie and Paul, who gave me my first sewing machine—

and Nick, who let me keep the nine or ninety that followed. I seem to have lost count.

To TW, DV, AF, DM for the Spark.

To Jessika Hepburn, Karen LePage, and Kimberly Kling—there is no doubt you'd risk your hide for me.

Eternally grateful for cupcakes and the Oh My! Handmade Goodness community.

To the Hanics and the Devers families.

To Roxane Cerda, Michele Fry, and everyone at C&T Publishing for sharing in my enthusiasm and clocking endless hours to see it through.

To Britta Folden, Seth Godin, Lori-Ann Claurhout. To Turnkey Enterprises, Alice Voss-Kantor, Jo Leichte. And to Pino's Pizza delivery.

CONTENTS

INTRODUCTION

How wonderful that no one need wait

a single moment to improve the world.

— Anne Frank —

You've taken the first step to help change the world. Armed with a pair of scissors and a pile of unwanted, outgrown, stained, or ripped T-shirts, together we are changing the way we consume and create. Whether you are looking for ways to reuse creatively, learning to sew, adopting eco-friendly habits, or trying to save money—the T-shirt revolution wants you. I've written this book as a pair of goggles that I hope will inspire you to look at things differently. Today we'll start with T-shirts, but tomorrow maybe you will seek ways to shift the status quo, freely express your inner desires, and make the world a better place through art.

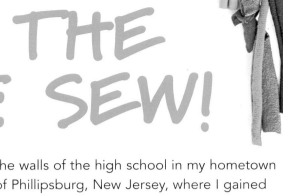

SAVE THE PLANET: SEW!

I can still remember the day I fell in love with sewing. Frustration had me standing in front of my cleared-off kitchen table, staring at a boxed-up Brother sewing machine. I was tired of shopping for little boys' clothing when I walked into every store and faced the same lackluster options. I wanted instead to design clothes for their quirky personalities (and to match their cloth diapers!). So I gathered up different materials I could find around the house, took a deep breath, and promised myself I was going to give sewing another try.

Yes, another try. The love hadn't come on my first attempt. My previous experience had left me with thread nests and a few broken needles—but I had been all too stubborn to read any instruction manual. This time I was ready. I set out to repurpose or upcycle some clothing for my two little boys, and a few short hours later I emerged victorious—with enough time to clear off the table and prepare for dinner!

Growing kids meant that a donation pile was always in progress: prime for picking fabrics where I would find just the right colors or patterns to use on whimsical appliqués right at home. Talk about convenience! As friends and family took notice, they began dropping off their unwanted clothes and requesting custom clothing for their kids too!

Sewing evolved into a passion of mine, but this story begins even before then. It was within the walls of the high school in my hometown of Phillipsburg, New Jersey, where I gained interest in all things agricultural, filling my class schedule with landscaping courses, animal science, and environmental education. I even picked up a part-time job on a local dairy farm. Did you know that a cow has four stomachs? It's true. I was intrigued and empowered by the direct connection that the agriculture sciences have on our economy, environment, and communities. Paired with my love for the outdoors, I pursued an environmental science major in college. My dream was to become a park ranger or teacher, so I could inspire younger generations to foster a connection with the natural world and responsible actions to sustain it.

These deep-rooted values are at the core of my sewing philosophy. I know firsthand the effects of our consumption and waste. Our daily choices impact future generations in ways we don't often think about. For instance, today the United States has 1,900 active municipal solid waste landfills. Within the next 20 years all of them will be full. What happens then?

I spent a lot of time honing my craft and mastering different aspects of sewing before launching my own clothing line, TrashN2Tees, in 2010. Every original design is made from 100% reclaimed materials. I joke that I've found a way to combine all the loves of my life and call it a day job. But really, it's true.

Sewing with a Purpose

Soon the TrashN2Tees blog was started. There, I began to share tips and tutorials to encourage and inspire others to consume less and recycle more. Although many of us cut up shirts to use as cleaning rags around the house, an alarming 11.1 million tons of textiles are discarded each year in the United States alone.

The numbers are staggering. The average person in the United States throws nearly 70 pounds of clothing into our landfills every single year. The Environmental Protection Agency says that 95% of this could be reused or recycled. I say that 100% can be creatively repurposed! I know that if I can teach people to sew, sharing tutorials, tips, and ideas to reimagine our waste, we can have an enormous impact.

Also, used clothing can be recycled into industrial rags, used in car seat insulation and sound-proofing material, or even shredded and respun into new cloth. Unfortunately, reliable local programs are not widely available, but some nonprofits accept used clothing and resell what they can't use to textile recyclers.

In 2011, I offered a mail-in rebate incentive and in doing so helped divert nearly 2,000 pounds of clothing from our landfills. In 2012, I launched a large-scale clothing recycling program that spans from the Midwest to the northeastern United States, and together we've collectively diverted more than 72 tons of clothing (equivalent to 404,407 T-shirts!) from our landfills. Even if you make only one project from this book, you are a part of that growing number. Can I count on you for T-shirt number 404,408? Why not invite a friend over and create together (404,409)! Just like that we can continue to grow our movement.

Today, locations nationwide participate in TrashN2Tees clothing recycling. You can find the nearest location by visiting trashn2tees.com.

Why T-Shirts?

You might not have a donation pile from a pair of kids with super growing powers at home, or a third-floor studio space with 200 pounds of T-shirts, but T-shirts are everywhere—and sometimes even for free! If we peek inside any closet or drawer, we are bound to find at least one unworn T-shirt. We're more likely to find a dozen. After you've checked your own bottom drawer, ask friends and family for any shirts they might be waiting to turn into rags, and scout around for promotional tees at local events. If you're still on the hunt, T-shirts can be purchased for anywhere from 25 cents to $2.50; head to your nearest thrift store or stop by your neighborhood yard sales—meccas for T-shirt hunters. Scope out online sites, such as ThredUP, Craigslist, and eBay, for secondhand clothing. Keep in mind that small stains, rips, and cracked screen printing graphics or logos are welcome; we're not simply refashioning these shirts but reinventing them into usable fabric. After you get your newly acquired stash home, be sure to run everything through the wash.

You'll need one or more T-shirts for most of the projects in this book, but I've included some small, quick, and scrappy ideas. My aim is to use everything that we cut up! And cotton jersey knit, the type of fabric that T-shirts are made from, is easy to work with—another reason I use T-shirts.

The Beauty of Jersey Knit

- It's easy to sew. (See Sewing with Knits, page 20.)

- It doesn't fray. You can leave your edge cuts unfinished for a casual look.

- It's low maintenance. It's washable, doesn't always require ironing, and is easier to care for than other apparel fabrics.

- When cut, jersey knit tends to curl on the edge, which is handy for making drawstrings.

- It's stretchy and warm, and comfortable to wear.

- It's absorbent.

The Life Cycle of a T-Shirt

Do you have a favorite T-shirt? If you're like most of us, you have more than one! They're neatly tucked into drawers—commemorating marathons, emblazed with logos, celebrating family reunions, or promoting your favorite local restaurant. I still have T-shirts in my closet from when I was in school! **Have you ever thought about the impact "the life" of just one shirt has on the environment?**

The life cycle of all clothing has five major stages: the material, production, shipping, use, and disposal.

According to a study published in 2009, the material, production, and transportation of a single T-shirt weighing 6 ounces uses 700 gallons of water, 0.22 pounds of fertilizer, and 1.2 pounds of fossil fuels. That's just for one shirt!

1. The material phase includes farming, irrigating, fertilizing, harvesting, and ginning. Although cotton is a natural fiber, it still takes a toll on the environment. About 25% of all pesticides in the United States are used on cotton crops.

2. After the cotton is grown and harvested, it moves along into the production phase. This is spinning, knitting, wet processing, bleaching, dyeing, confection (the mixing of different fibers), cutting, and sewing—and all of these require energy. Additionally, dyes and bleaches are harmful pollutants and can contaminate water sources.

3. After the T-shirt is manufactured, it enters the transportation phase. As you might guess, this is where the shirts are shipped out to warehouses for distribution. This usually involves overseas shipping. Check your tags. Are most of your cotton shirts made in China or India?

4. Then the shirt reaches the retail market, where it can be purchased, and thus enters into the use phase. Maybe this seems like the least detrimental phase of the T-shirt life cycle, but take into consideration the number of times you've washed and dried it. It's estimated that every household does nearly 400 loads of laundry per year, using about 40 gallons of water per full load (with a conventional washer.)

5. Finally, the life cycle is completed in the disposal phase. This could involve incineration, a process that releases harmful toxic emissions into our air. Alternately a shirt that ends up in the landfill will take years to break down.

Remarkable, huh? But a lot of things can be done to decrease the damage inflicted on the environment just because we have to dress. **Reuse and recycle clothes.** I will show you some ways to do this throughout the pages of this book.

Tips to Save the Planet

Pick a project in this book to make.

Donate clothes to charities or organizations that recycle textiles.

When possible, buy secondhand or organic clothing.

Turn down the thermostat on your washer and hang the laundry to dry when the weather permits.

If your clothes are too ragged or worn out to wear, cut them up and use them as cleaning rags.

My Style

Though I no longer have to unbox my sewing machine and put it away again each day, I am still learning and experimenting. I love to do that! I believe that perfection is boring. When I finally get to sit down in front of my beloved Bernina, I employ a laid-back, less-calculating freestyle to my sewing. I love diving into a new project headfirst and making my way as I go along. All of the projects in this book can be tweaked a little this way or that; don't feel pressured to have exact measurements (just try to get pretty close), and feel free to resize them to fit your needs. My hope is that you are as continually inspired by the idea as I am, that our humble hands can take something that we were ready to trash and transform it into a beautiful wearable or practical work of art.

THE BASICS

Deconstructing a T-Shirt

Throughout this book I will use terms and techniques that will allow us to deconstruct a T-shirt (or any other shirt) to get the largest amount of workable material. Familiarize yourself with the parts of your T-shirt.

The *hem* is the finished edge on the bottom of a T-shirt and on the ends of sleeves. The fabric is folded under about an inch or so and sewn into place. In the projects Drawstring Sleeve Bag (page 115) and Reusable Produce Bag (page 119), we actually take advantage of the existing hem to make reusable bags. This is one way I try to maximize existing characteristics of a garment to practical reuse.

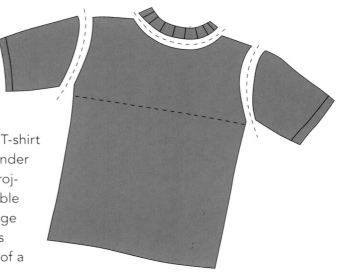

Terms to Know

APPLIQUÉ   Stitched by hand or machine, appliqué is a method of applying a piece of fabric on top of another piece of fabric.

BASTING   Stitching used to hold two pieces of fabric together before sewing with a more permanent stitch. If done using your machine, use the longest stitch setting.

BATTING   Used in quiltmaking, this material is the middle layer between the top and bottom fabrics.

BIAS   The 45° angle that runs diagonally across the lengthwise piece of fabric.

FABRIC GRAIN   The lengthwise or crosswise thread in woven fabric. If you take a close look at your fabric, you'll see the threads run in two directions. This is the grain. With jersey knit materials (or your T-shirts) you will notice that the stitches on the right side of the fabric make columns similar to a pattern you might find on a knitted sweater.

INTERFACING   A material that is either sewn into or ironed between fabrics to add structure and stability.

NOTIONS   A tool or accessory for sewing—pins, zippers, thread, or anything used for a project that is not the fabric.

SEAM ALLOWANCE   The measurement that extends past the sewing line. In the United States this measurement is usually expressed in fractions of an inch.

Tools

My time is precious and best spent sneaking in cuddles with my family along the way. I don't have the space or energy to invest in an expansive tool kit, so over the years I've narrowed it down to the basics. You can make nearly everything in this book with just a pair of scissors, a T-shirt, and a needle with thread. Certain products help make swift progress of your T-shirt crafting, such as a rotary cutter, straight-edge ruler, and cutting mat. And of course, a sewing machine.

Along with sharing some techniques that can be used to customize your fabric, tips for sewing jersey knit (T-shirts), and skill-building practices, I am going to break down what tools work best for each.

SCISSORS

Work best for cutting out patterns, cutting along curves, dissecting T-shirts (page 10), clipping curved seams, trimming loose threads.

Quite possibly one of the hardest-working tools in your arsenal, scissors are worth investing a little more money into so that you can get a good pair and dedicate it only to cutting fabrics. If you try to cut through T-shirts with any run-of-the-mill craft-box scissors, you'll find that the fabric gets wedged in the scissors and won't cut. Or if it does cut, the edges will be chewed up. I have a variety of sizes of scissors in my studio, and each one has its advantages. Most often I reach for a pair of spring-loaded Ginghers that will cut through several layers of fabric like butter. They are very well made (in Greensboro, North Carolina) and cut beautifully. They'll last you a lifetime if you get them sharpened occasionally and use them only to cut fabric. I also keep a smaller pair nearby for narrow cutouts in my appliqué work. For beginners, you can absolutely get by with a pair of shears.

tip > SHARP SCISSORS

Regular use of scissors for cutting fabrics will dull your blades. You can take a large piece of aluminum foil, fold it in half a couple of times, and cut through it multiple times to resharpen your scissors. To have them professionally resharpened costs around $7; services may be available at your local crafting store or quilt shop or a hardware store.

ROTARY CUTTER

Works best for large cuts, precise straight lines when used with ruler, cutting through several layers of fabric.

You might confuse this with a pizza cutter, but it's much sharper! Essentially it is a round razor-sharp blade with a handle. You roll over the fabric with it, and it cuts. Rotary cutters are available with different blade sizes and can fulfill a number of needs. A larger blade size means you can cut through more fabric faster. A 60mm blade is perfect for cutting yardage, while the 18mm is mostly used to make smaller cuts or to work around curves. I typically use my 45mm rotary cutter (every day!) partnered up with a ginormous self-healing mat and translucent 24″ nonslip ruler. It's the perfect size for doing both big and small cuts.

tips > ROTARY CUTTERS

To get the best use from your rotary cutter, use it with two other tools: a self-healing mat and straight-edge ruler. You'll have no problem finding them bundled together in kits at an affordable price.

The replaceable blades are recyclable, but why not trade them in for new ones? The L.P. Sharp Company (lpsharp.com) will exchange your blades for less than the usual cost of purchasing replacements. Their program allows you to send in a minimum of five blades of any brand, size, and condition in exchange for new Olfa brand or generic blades.

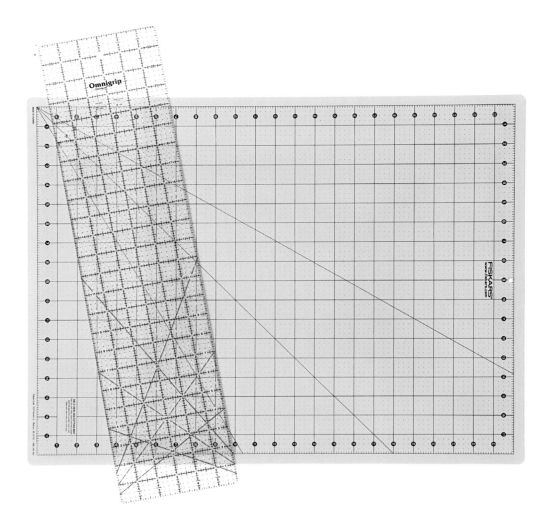

SELF-HEALING CUTTING MAT

Works best for providing a flat surface to work on, keeping your tabletops from getting cut.

In addition to protecting your table or floor from cut marks, a cutting mat can be used to mark angles and other measurements when cutting out fabrics. They generally have measurements, just like a ruler, and grid lines. I recommend getting the largest mat that can fit your workspace. Keep in mind that if it does not have a dedicated place, the mat must be stored lying flat or upright; it can't be rolled or stored like a band poster.

Self-healing mats appear to seal themselves up after each pass of the rotary blade. They are made of some mystery material, a PVC vinyl composite. Eventually, particularly with heavy use, they'll stop "healing," but until then, they provide a continuously smooth surface to cut on!

NONSLIP RULER

Works best for making straight cuts on your fabric.

Nonslip is the important part here. Do not try to use a regular yardstick when cutting fabric with a rotary cutter. It most often will not end pretty. Nonslip rulers contain a special feature that resists slipping, so you can safely cut your fabric.

MARKING PEN

Used for tracing patterns or templates onto fabric. Here's an über-thrifty reuse tip perfect for those times you can't find anything else to use: save the small bits of soap bars and use them as marking chalk.

SEAM RIPPER

With any luck you won't need this too often, but it's entirely okay if you do! Seam rippers are actually a great tool for deconstructing garments to upcycle. You don't have to pluck each stitch one by one—instead, slide the seam ripper under the stitches on one side of the seam. Do this every third or fourth stitch and you should be able to carefully pull the seam apart.

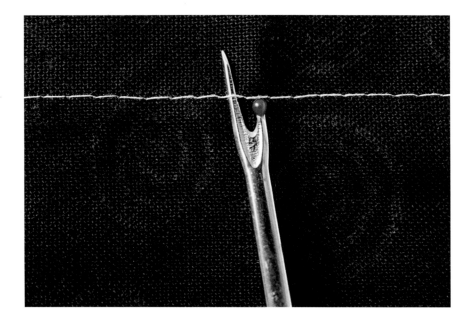

STRAIGHT PINS

Work best for keeping fabrics aligned.

Not everyone pins all the time when sewing, but pinning can be very helpful, especially when working with knit materials. A pin is a thin piece of metal with a sharp point at one end and a round head at the other. Pins temporarily fasten materials together. I'm not sure there is a right or wrong way to pin. Over the years I've seen it done in every way imaginable. My best practice is to place the pins parallel to the seamline as if they were stitches. Pinning the fabric this way helps prevent you from sewing over the pin, too!

tip > STITCHING OVER PINS?

When using a sewing machine it might seem like a good idea to sew over the pin—I do not recommend doing this. It's a gamble—sure, most of the time you'll stitch over the pin but if you don't you will break a needle or thread, and worst of all you can seriously damage your machine. Instead I like to keep a magnetic pin holder or shallow box to the right of my machine while I work. When sewing along my seam, I remove pins 1″ before I reach them and set them on the pin holder—never taking my eyes off the seam.

Also … not all pins are the same. There are pins specifically for quilting, dressmaking, and appliqué, just to name a few. The style of pins that work best is really a matter of preference. Try out a few styles before settling in. I found that I prefer to use straight pins with big bright balls on the heads. They're easy to grab and easy to see if you happen to drop one.

NEEDLES

Works best for … sewing!

These come in a variety of styles for many uses as well. For your machine, I recommend a stretch, ballpoint needle. This special needle is designed for sewing knit fabrics. A ballpoint needle has a slightly rounded tip that allows it to slip through the fibers of your T-shirt with less obvious punctures. It also prevents skipped stitches. You could also use a universal needle if that is what you have on hand. If you do, it's important to understand that as the needle punches through the woven jersey knit fabric, it creates tiny tears in the fabric that will likely get worse as you wash and wear. The same idea goes for picking up hand-sewing needles; you can use a multipurpose needle, but a ballpoint needle is best for jersey knit.

If your sewing machine has an option for zigzag, you most likely can use a twin (double) needle. Be sure to read your machine's manual for proper setup. This method is great for hems: it builds strength in your seams by creating two straight-stitch lines on top of the fabric with zigzag underneath.

MATERIALS

In addition to T-shirts, the following items will be needed for some projects.

Stuffing   Available in a variety of materials including organic cotton, cotton/poly blends, and recycled polyester batting is used to fill plush toys, pillows, or even seat cushions. You can purchase little tools or carefully use a chopstick or pencil end to help pack stuffing into place.

tip > STUFFING

The trick to good stuffing is to first push small puffs of filling into the corners and crannies before filling your main body.

Batting   This is flat stuffing that comes in rolls or precut sizes for easy use and can be used to make seat cushions or for quilting. You can find a variety of eco-friendly options available.

Interfacing   T-shirts are comfortable and cozy, but that doesn't always work out well when you are using them to craft something else entirely. Interfacing is an additional layer applied to the inside of fabric (most often used in garments or handbags) to add firmness, shape, structure, and support. In this book I recommend a variety of interfacings, including fusible or sew-in, woven or non-woven, and knit. They're available in light, medium, and heavy weights. In each project I'll specify the type of interfacing, used but you can choose to use any brand.

However, I am a fan of Pellon Sheer-Knit interfacing. It is silky soft, lightweight, and knit, which allows the T-shirt fabric to stay comfortable to wear. It can be applied with an iron. I use this for two reasons: Anytime I appliqué a design onto a T-shirt especially for babies, I will use the sheer knit to cover up any stitches on the inside of a finished shirt to create a smooth surface that is less likely to cause irritation. I also like to use it when I am patchworking with knit material. Jersey has a tendency to curl under, so this adds a little stability without bulk. It can be purchased by the yard in white or black.

Tip to Save the Planet

Quilters Dream Green is a soft, cozy batting made completely from recycled plastic bottles. Even the packaging is recyclable! Each pound of Dream Green batting keeps ten plastic bottles out of our landfills.

Fusible webbing

An adhesive material that fuses fabric to fabric or to another porous surface, such as wood or cardboard. It comes in a wide range of choices and can be purchased prepackaged or by the yard at your local craft store.

Tip to Save the Planet

Substitute upcycled flannel (cut from your favorite lumberjack shirts) in place of lightweight or midweight interfacing. Not only does it offer a great amount of support, but it's still soft and helps to reduce even more clothing going into our landfills!

Hand Stitches

No matter how quickly technology progresses, hand sewing will always have a place. It's a fine art that I have yet to master. I usually resort to a running stitch, but other common and good-to-know stitches include the backstitch and whipstitch. Pick your favorite. A couple of projects also call for you to do a ladder stitch.

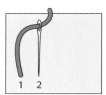 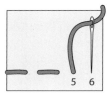

Running stitch

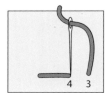 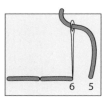 

Backstitch

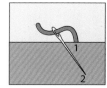 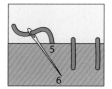

Whipstitch

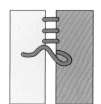

Ladder stitch

Customizing Your Fabric

I'm the type of maker who doesn't waste time mocking up an idea and instead jumps in head-first. Yes, sometimes it doesn't always turn out as I planned, but I love that risk. Failure only provides me with a new opportunity to re-create and serves me well for gaining new skills and insights. Embrace the idea that a slightly miscalculated cut or slip of the paintbrush will not be the end to your finished product. Armed with the basics, I hope that you're inspired to follow your own instincts along the way and design something never before seen.

Customizing your experience along the way is a great way to let your unique personality come through in your works of art. You might find yourself wandering the aisles of the thrift store just about to pull your hair out looking for the perfect T-shirt. Why not make it yourself? Taking discarded materials and turning them into a one-of-a-kind masterpiece is fun and easy.

Dyeing and Painting

Dyeing T-shirts to any color you can imagine is as easy as adding salt, water, and a packet of dye into your washing machine. With the help of fabric markers and paints we can design knit material unlike anything in the stores by using things we already have around the house to create patterns and geometric shapes or to use as stencils.

Rummage through your junk drawer, check the fridge for leftovers, or take a walk outside to find inspiration. Use toilet paper rolls to stamp circles. Create your stamp by cutting out a simple shape from foam and mounting it on a solid surface. Paint an ear of corn and then make prints by rolling it over your fabric. Painter's tape can be used to make plaid.

Appliqué

Appliqué literally means "to put on" in French (oh là là—you just said something fancy!) and is a technique used to decorate the surface of fabric by applying one or more pieces of cut fabric on top of another fabric. Using T-shirts along with fusible interfacing, you can create no-sew appliqué by simply using a hot iron or sew your finished design down using a machine stitch or embroidery stitches. Designs can be as complex or simple as you like.

Appliqué is used in the Cuff Bracelets (page 82), Deer Plushies (page 69), and Reversible Dog Shirt (page 88) projects in this book.

How to Appliqué

The type of fusible webbing you use is up to you. You'll be able to buy this either in packaged sheets or off the bolt at your local craft or fabric store. Both sides are generally covered with removable paper or film.

To get started, trace your design, in reverse, onto the paper backing using a Sharpie marker or pencil.

Cut out the general shape, leaving 2″ excess around the design, and remove the paper backing from the side without the traced design.

Place your cutout onto the wrong side of the appliqué fabric and press with an iron as directed in the product instructions. Allow to cool and then cut out the traced shape. Cutting too soon can

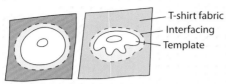

T-shirt fabric
Interfacing
Template

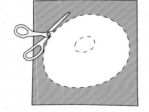

cause your trusty scissors to get gunked up with glue residue over time.

Now it's time to apply your design. Remove the paper backing and position in place. When you're happy with the placement, iron to set it as directed on your main fabric (T-shirt, pillowcase, etc.). Many fusible web brands require no sewing and if gently cared for will not peel off. Some products promise no sewing required, but my best practice is to always sew the appliqué down.

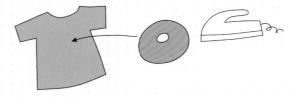

Using a sewing machine or embroidery stitches, finish the edges as desired.

How to Use Patterns and Templates

As I mentioned earlier, time is of the essence when it comes to my sewing. I'm going to take a guess that it might be the same for you too. Anytime I create patterns for appliqué designs or to be used with fusible webbing (which you will be doing throughout the majority of this book), I will trace the object directly onto the webbing using disappearing ink, a pen, a Sharpie—whatever is in arm's reach. Patterns to make the templates can be resized using a home scanner or your local print or office supply store.

Sewing with Knits

Imagine my surprise when I talk to people who are afraid to sew knits! I never realized that it was considered fussy or difficult. When all of this began, I just dove headfirst into my pile of tees and figured it out along the way. There was a sense of confidence in knowing that the shirt I was cutting up and sewing could be replaced for just $1. On the other hand, I was petrified of sewing with woven cotton. Fraying edges, special stitches, and $8 or more a yard! Talk about high maintenance.

Over the years I picked up a few tips and tricks—many of which we use in this book. They will help you manipulate knits and conquer sewing with them without a bunch of fancy tools or machines.

NEEDLE   Whether you are sewing by hand or machine, outfit yourself with the correct needle—ballpoint needles (sometimes called stretch or jersey needles) are the best for knitted fabrics, but universal needles will also work. (See Tools, page 11.)

THREAD   Use an all-purpose polyester or cotton-covered polyester thread. The polyester content allows for a bit of stretch.

Tip to Save the Planet
If you can find it, Gütermann makes a 100% recycled polyester thread called Sew-all Thread 100 m rPET.

CURLING   When piecing a pattern together and constructing a garment, the edges of jersey knit fabric can be hard to align because the material tends to curl up. Use a clear, washable glue stick to tack the edges together; readjust until they are lined up perfectly. This can also be used to help keep two pieces of knit (or any other shifty fabrics) together if you do not have a walking foot attachment. Interfacing or spray starch and an iron also help to stabilize knit materials.

STRETCHING AND PUCKERING   What is this *walking foot* I speak of? It's a special attachment for your sewing machine— and if you have to purchase one, it's worth the investment. The walking foot helps the feed dogs on the sewing machine move multiple layers of material through the machine together without shifting apart. This helps prevent puckers, twisting, and stretching of your knit material as you sew.

Let the feed dogs and walking foot do their job; don't pull the fabric, which stretches it, or push so much that you ruffle it. It's easy to forget this if you are used to sewing with material with less give. Evenly feed fabric through the machine to avoid distortion of your finished project. And go slowly.

SERGER MACHINES OR ZIGZAG STITCHES are brought into any discussion about sewing with knits. They're used to help secure seams and prevent stitches from breaking when the fabric is stretched. Many of the projects in *The Upcycled T-Shirt* are made using a straight stitch. This works well for us because many of the projects we make will not have a lot of stress on the seams. However, for wearables, I recommend you increase the length of your straight stitch; this will give it more flexibility.

Making Yardage

Use your old and ready-to-discard T-shirts to create yards of fabric for any sewing or crafting project. Use a ¼″ seam allowance. Here are two methods.

Patchwork Method

1. Cut even squares or rectangles from shirts. (The Summer Flounce Dress, page 28, is made from 8″ × 12″ rectangles.)

2. With right sides together, using a narrow zigzag stitch or a serger, sew rectangles (or squares) together along 1 long edge.

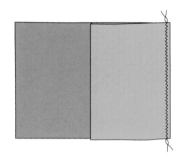

3. Continue piecing a new rectangle to the previous set until desired yardage width is reached.

tip >

You can also place the pieces wrong sides together using either method to allow the seams to show and be part of the design element. But choose a method and stick with it for a single project.

4. Begin the next row in the same manner.

5. When a new row of the same width is created, stitch it to the previously constructed fabric until the desired fabric yardage length is achieved.

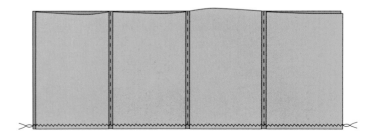

Strip-Piecing Method

1. Cut strips at least 2½˝ wide and as long as you can.

2. With right sides together, using a narrow zigzag stitch or a serger, sew strips together along 1 long edge.

3. Continue piecing a new strip to the strip set until the desired yardage width is reached.

4. When the desired fabric width is reached, trim the bottom edge even. (This is easiest to do with a quilting ruler or straight edge, a rotary cutter, and a cutting mat.)

If you need a longer length, make rows and connect them end to end until you reach the desired length.

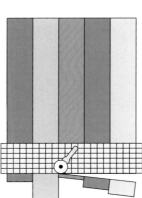

Yardage Cheat Sheet

(Approximations)

For yardage:

    1 large T-shirt = ⅝ yard of fabric when pieced together

    1 X-large T-shirt = ¾ yard of fabric when pieced together

For T-shirt yarn:

    1 large T-shirt = 15 yards of 1½˝-wide T-shirt yarn

    1 yard of 60˝-wide jersey knit fabric = 35 yards of 2˝-wide T-shirt yarn

Making Yarn

Method 1: Easy Way

1. Spread a T-shirt on your cutting mat. Flatten out any creases, as they'll create a jagged inconsistency in your yarn.

2. Fold in half widthwise—put the side edges of your T-shirt together and the sleeves together.

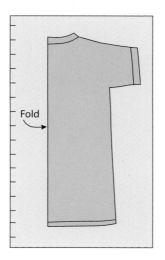

Fold

3. Place a straight-edged ruler just above the bottom hemline. Cut completely through all 4 layers using a rotary cutter. When you pick up this fabric it is a loop that you can cut to the desired length.

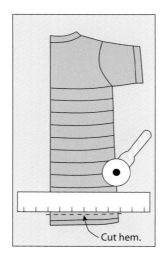

Cut hem.

4. Measure up from the last cut to the desired width of yarn you'd like. I prefer to cut mine 1½″–2″; this general size, after being pulled taut, is the perfect diameter for draw-strings, packaging details, and headbands.

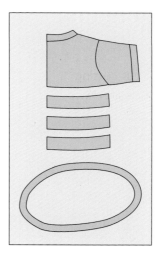

tip >

For the best T-shirt yarn, use

T-shirts that have no side seams.

Method 2: Continuous

1. Lay out a T-shirt on a work surface. Cut a horizontal line directly under the sleeves. Also cut off the hem on the bottom of the shirt. You need only the middle section for this project. Put the top and bottom pieces into your scrap pile.

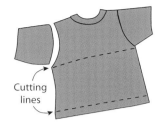

Cutting lines

2. Place the shirt section on your table with the open edges at the left and right and the folded edges at the top and bottom. Fold 1 side edge of the T-shirt toward the other, leaving a 2″ space at the top. Smooth the T-shirt out. It doesn't need to be perfect, but large creases can give the strips jagged, inconsistent edges.

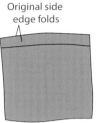

Original side edge folds

Fold at bottom.

3. Without cutting the space at the top, cut the fabric into strips of desired width. Be sure to cut completely through the 4 layers of material, stopping just after the side edge that you've folded up. (In other words, you do not want to cut the 2″ space at the top!)

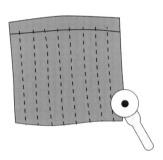

4. Carefully unfold the T-shirt so you can see the separate strips. Begin cutting the strips diagonally across at the top 2″ that are still connected. Starting at the first strip, cut diagonally to the second strip. Repeat across.

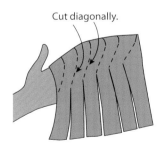

Cut diagonally.

5. Now that you have a single strip of T-shirt yarn, pull it through your hands to create the tube shape. This enables the edges to curl.

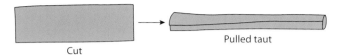

Cut — Pulled taut

6. Keep pulling until it is all tube-shaped.

One men's size Large T-shirt yields about 14 yards of T-shirt yarn in 1½″–2″ strips.

In this book you'll find several ways to put your yarn to use, including the Arm Knit Throw (page 55), Seat Cushion (page 62), Reusable Produce Bags (page 119), and Macramé Plant Hanger (page 64)—but also know that T-shirt yarn can be used in favorite crochet or knitting projects that call for bulky yarns. Scrappy strands of T-shirt yarn that are left behind will be perfect for surprising your furry friends with treats of their own! (See Pet Toys, page 86.)

Joining Yarn Strips

I created a single strand of T-shirt yarn using a series of slipknots from short scrappy strips.

1. After cutting all of the strips to the desired width and length, make a small snip cut on both ends.

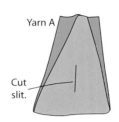

Yarn A

Cut slit.

2. With 2 strips at hand, take a strip (yarn B) and pass it through a slit in the other (yarn A).

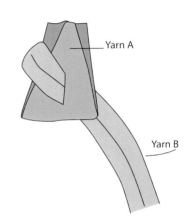

Yarn A

Yarn B

3. Take the beginning end of the yarn B strip and feed it through the slit in the opposite end of the yarn B strip. Pull tight.

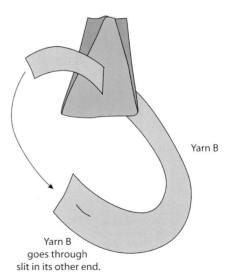

Yarn B

Yarn B goes through slit in its other end.

SUMMER FLOUNCE DRESS

SUMMER FLOUNCE DRESS *Cloud-soft, pajama-comfortable, and especially sassy thanks to the flounce,* this dress may be your favorite by the time summer ends. Pair with a cardigan for fireside wear, or wear it every day to and from the beach.*

* A flounce is strip of decorative, usually gathered or pleated material attached to an edge of a garment.

❯ YOU'LL NEED

3 yards of 54˝ jersey or interlock knit fabric *or* approximately 6 extra large T-shirts made into yardage (page 22)

Coordinating thread

Marking tools (chalk or chalk pen, etc.)

T-shirt yarn—enough to wrap around your waist twice

Change will not come if we wait for some other person, or if we wait for some other time. We are the ones we've been waiting for. We are the change that we seek.

— Barack Obama —

Finished Size	XS	S	M	L	XL
Bodice measurement at bust	35½˝	37½˝	39½˝	42½˝	45˝
Skirt measurement at hip	53˝	56˝	58˝	61˝	65˝

Prep

1. Using the patterns (pullout pages P1 and P2), cut:

1 Bodice Front (on fold) • 1 Bodice Back (on fold)

2 Skirt (both on fold) • 2 Flounce

2. Press a crease to mark the center front (CF) and center back (CB) of all the pieces. (Alternatively, mark each CF and CB with a chalk pen, or make a tiny clip in the seam allowance.)

3. Cut a 2˝-wide strand of T-shirt yarn twice your waist measurement. (See Making Yarn, page 24.)

Sew

All seam allowances are ¼″ unless otherwise indicated. Use a serger or a narrow zigzag stitch 3.0 long × 1.5 wide.

1. With right sides together (or wrong sides together for a raw-edged look), stitch the front and back together at the shoulder seams.

2. To add the flounce neckline, place the wrong side of the flounce to the right side of the bodice front. Pin the inside edge of the flounce to the neckline edge of front, trying to avoid stretching the neckline edge. If the flounce is longer than the neckline, trim off the extra fabric. Stitch in place.

3. Repeat Step 2 for the bodice back.

4. With right sides together (or wrong sides together for a raw-edge look), sew the bodice front to the bodice back at the side seams.

5. Turn the armhole edges under ¼″ to the wrong side. Zigzag in place.

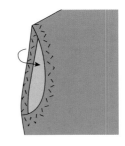

6. With right sides together (or wrong sides together for a raw-edge look), sew together the front skirt to the back skirt at the side seams.

7. Attach the bodice to the skirt, right sides together (or wrong sides together for a raw-edge look), with a ¾″ seam allowance. Press the seam allowances toward the top.

Stitch ¾″ seam.

8. Make 2 small slits in the seam allowance, the first ¾″ to the left and the second ¾″ to the right of the center front.

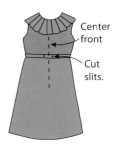

Center front

Cut slits.

9. Topstitch the seam allowances to the bodice, forming a casing for the drawstring waist.

10. Using a safety pin (or bodkin, if you have one), thread the T-shirt yarn through the casing you made in Step 9. Tie a couple knots in the ends of the jersey drawstring.

Topstitch seam allowance.

YOUR NEW FAVORITE HOODIE

YOUR NEW FAVORITE HOODIE *The name of this one says it all. Just wrap yourself in comfort, and then head out on an adventure! Whether you're hitting the trails, heading to yoga, or carpooling to practice, you'll love the cowl neck that converts to a hood.*

⌐> YOU'LL NEED

2¼ yards knit fabric (see Making Yardage, page 22) or 4 T-shirts

90/14 or 80/12 ballpoint or stretch needle

Coordinating thread

Marking tool

Prep

If Using Yardage

1. Use the patterns (pullout pages P1 and P2) to cut:

> 1 Front Body (on fold)
>
> 1 Back Body (on fold)
>
> 2 Sleeves
>
> 2 Hood or Cowl pieces

2. Prepare the pieces by pressing each in half to mark center front (CF) and center back (CB) or center (C).

Now you're ready to sew.

If Using T-Shirts

1. Cut the neck ribbing plus 1″ from a baggy T-shirt to create a large neck opening.

2. From each of 2 women's small T-shirts, cut a piece 14″ (or so) up from hem, preserving the hem edges. (This is for the hood/cowl.)

3. Prepare the pieces by pressing each in half to mark center front (CF) and center back (CB) or center (C).

4. Cut the hood/cowl pieces 1″ smaller than the circumference of the main body neckline. Stitch them together to form a tube.

5. Follow Sew, Steps 7 and 8 (pages 34 and 35), to add the hood/cowl to your shirt. Follow Sew, Step 9 (page 35), for an optional pocket.

Sew

All seam allowances are ⅜˝. Use a stretchy stitch on your machine or a serger. Narrow zigzag (3.0 long × 1.5 wide) is great if you don't have fancy stitch options.

1. With right sides together, stitch the body front to the body back at the shoulders. Press the seam allowances toward the back. Topstitch the seam allowances to hold in place.

2. Pin the center of sleeve cap to the shoulder seam, with right sides together. Pin at each underarm end. Stitch the sleeve cap to the shirt. Press the seam allowances toward the sleeve.

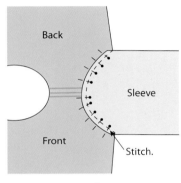

Back

Sleeve

Front

Stitch.

3. With right sides together, pin the underarm seam, the sleeve hem edge, and the shirt hem edge. Stitch from the wrist to the shirt hem in 1 pass.

Side seam

4. Press the seam allowances toward the back. Stitch a square in the armpit area to hold all the seam allowances in place.

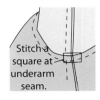

Stitch a square at underarm seam.

5. Repeat Steps 2–4 for the other sleeve. You can stop here and have a hoodless shirt. Continue with Steps 6–9 to add the hood/cowl.

6. Stitch the hood/cowl pieces into tubes along the short side of each.

7. Place the hood/cowl pieces wrong sides together, matching CF and CB and sides. Stitch together ½˝ from the raw edges (the edges will curl a bit, like the shirt and sleeve raw edges) or along the previous hem stitching of the T-shirts.

Stitch.

Center front

8. Slide the hood/cowl into the T-shirt body, with right sides together, and pin along the neckline through the body and the

2 unstitched layers of the cowl. Stitch, stretching the cowl slightly while stitching to distribute it evenly along the neckline of shirt. Press the seam allowances toward the shirt. Topstitch the seam allowance to shirt.

9. You can add a pocket to the front by cutting a piece of T-shirt about 9″ × 9″. Pin the bottom edge of the pocket about 4″ above the hoodie's

Optional pocket

hem, and then topstitch the top and bottom edges of the pocket.

tip >

You can make a shirt from yardage without a hood, too. There are several ways to make the neck edge—you can choose to keep the original neckline from the T-shirt you started with, or cut the neckline and then turn ¼˝ to the inside and stitch it, or cut the neckline and leave the raw edge as is. Get creative with your sleeves with multiple shirt pieces and a length of your choosing, too.

Short Sleeve? Long Sleeve?

1. If you'd like to make the sleeves longer, cut 2 rectangles from another T-shirt. First measure around the bottom edge of the existing sleeve on your T-shirt hoodie. Add ½˝ and this will be the width of the sleeve extension. The length will be the distance from the existing sleeve hem to your wrist plus ½˝—or however long you'd like the extended sleeve to be.

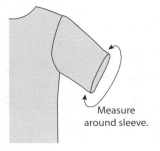

Measure around sleeve.

Distance around sleeve + ½˝

Distance from sleeve to wrist + ½˝

2. Stitch the sleeve extensions into a tube shape by pinning the long edges right sides together and stitch. Press the seam allowances open and turn right side out.

3. Slide each sleeve tube into the existing sleeve so that the sleeve extension and sleeve edge meet. Stitch along the existing sleeve hem edge. Pull the sleeve extension out and top-stitch around the original sleeve finished edge to hold the extension in place.

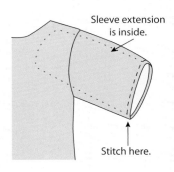

Sleeve extension is inside.

Stitch here.

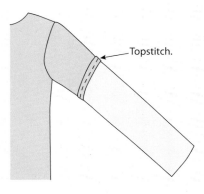

Topstitch.

T-SHIRT SHARD JEWELRY

T-SHIRT SHARD JEWELRY *Each time I cut up a T-shirt, it's inevitable that some amount of scrap is left behind. It might be just the bottom hemline or an entire top half of a shirt. Scrap busting became an art when I learned that my textile recycler wouldn't accept any pieces smaller than 6″ × 6″. What can be done with tiny pieces of material? I store all the bits, bobs, and doodads left behind in color-coded drawers and clear plastic jewelry-making boxes. They're used for small appliqué designs such as a dinosaur eye, bacon-shaped pins, or maybe a back wart on a goblin. I began to challenge myself to design projects and products that used the smallest pieces of material. This is how T-shirt shard jewelry came along.*

Hoop Earrings

⌐▸ YOU'LL NEED
Scrap T-shirt fabric

25mm earring hoops

Prep

1. Use whatever size scrap material you have on hand. Place it flat on a cutting mat surface. Square off the edges using a rotary cutter and ruler.

2. Make ⅜″ cuts vertically across the fabric.

3. Next, make ⅜″ cuts horizontally across the fabric. When finished you'll have ⅜″ × ⅜″ squares.

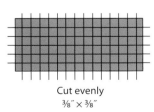

Cut evenly
⅜″ × ⅜″

4. Repeat until all the scraps are cut.

5. Hold the earring hoop in 1 hand and push the wire through the center of your  T-shirt shard. You may have to gently shimmy the fabric on the hoop. Do your best to push it between the knit threads for the least resistance.

6. Continue adding T-shirt shards to your earring wire until you are satisfied.

Teardrop Earrings

↱ YOU'LL NEED

Scrap T-shirt fabric (2 patterns or colors)

2 fishhook earring wires

2 jump rings, 4mm

Pellon Clear-Fuse

Needle-nose pliers

Prep

1. Square up 2 scrap fabrics. Each piece needs to be about 3″ square.

2. Cut Clear-Fuse the same size as your squares and iron to the wrong side of the squares.

Tip to Save the Planet

When your tees, scraps, and shards are so far gone that it seems nothing more can be done with them, shred them and mix the shredded material with polyfill stuffing for soft toys.

3. Allow the Clear-Fuse to cool down for 60 seconds before peeling the plastic film and removing it from the material.

NOTE: It can sometimes be tricky to peel up the film from a corner. Use a pin or scissors to gently catch and lift up the edge, or score the backing lightly with a pin and peel it up.

Remove backing from film.

4. Match the scrap fabric wrong sides together and iron. This will permanently bond them together.

5. Using a rotary cutter and straight edge, cut 2 strips 2″ × ¼″ each.

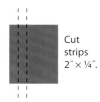

Cut strips 2″ × ¼″.

6. Use the needle-nose pliers to pry open a jump ring slightly. Fold a strip in half, short edges together, and hold the top between your fingers, creating a teardrop shape.

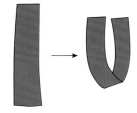

7. Push the open end of the jump ring through the center of the 2 touching ends.

8. Feed the jump ring through the bottom of the fishhook earring wire. Use the needle-nose pliers to close and secure your jump ring in place.

Pendant Necklace

> YOU'LL NEED

Scrap T-shirt fabric

Pellon Peltex I Ultra Firm

Pellon Clear-Fuse

Needle and thread

Jewelry findings (chain, bails, jump rings)

E600 adhesive or hot glue gun

Tip to Save the Planet

You can substitute cardboard, such as from a cereal box, for the Peltex in this project.

Prep

1. Cut T-shirt material (a front and back piece) and Clear-Fuse to the same size. Fold your Peltex in half and cut desired pendant shape. This will give you 2 exact shapes. My pendants are approximately 2″. I tested different shapes including teardrops, rectangles, hearts, and circles.

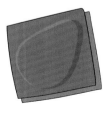

2. Press Clear-Fuse to the wrong side of each piece of T-shirt material, following directions. Let cool and remove the clear plastic film before proceeding to Step 3.

3. Stack both Peltex shapes on top of each other and place onto the wrong side of 1 piece of fabric.

4. Cover with a second layer of fabric, right side up, and press.

5. Use the needle and thread to sew around the shape. (See Hand Stitches, page 17.)

6. Cut out the pendant shape, leaving ⅛″ around your hand stitches.

7. Finish the pendant by attaching either a jump ring or a bail to the back.

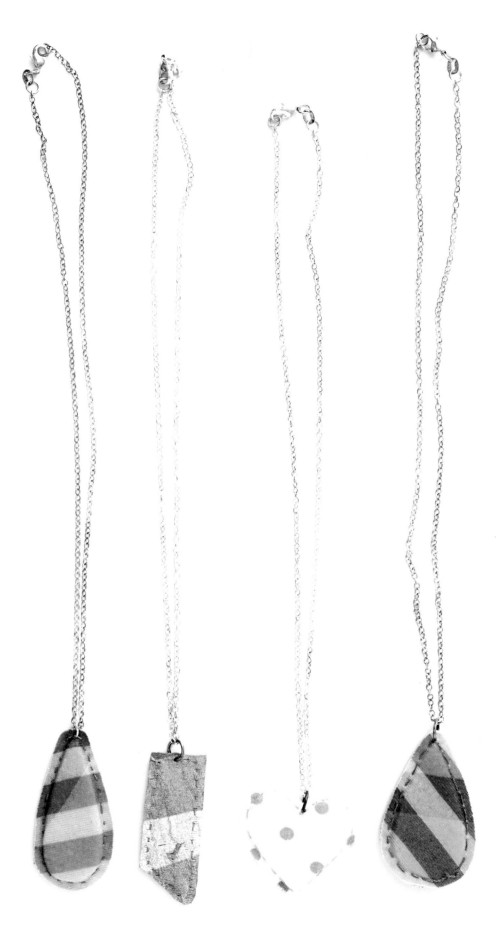

tips >

I love the jump ring
because it offers a little
more versatility.

You can use two
colors of fabric for a
reversible pendant.

MEN'S NECKTIE *Take your necktie outside the box, or cubicle. Show off your personality, support your favorite team, or wear your kids' artwork with a T-shirt tie. If rocking a half-Windsor is your style, this one's for you!*

➤ YOU'LL NEED

2 large or extra large T-shirts

1½ yards of sheerweight fusible interfacing (such as Pellon 906F)

Serger (*optional*)

Prep

1. Copy, trace, or cut out the pattern pieces (pullout page P1).

NOTE: This pattern is drafted for the average Joe. If your mister happens to be taller than 5′9″, you can adjust the pattern where indicated on piece 2.

2. Each pattern piece should be cut from the T-shirt on a 45° angle. This is the best way to fit all of your pattern pieces onto a shirt. (It's also known as cutting on the bias.) Pay attention to where existing screen prints will fall. One T-shirt will be used for the main fabric (front); the other will be used as the lining (back).

3. I find it easier to remove the section of T-shirt I am using before transferring the pattern. Cut up 1 side, around the arm seams, and under the neck band.

4. I like to cut my fusible interfacing pieces first and iron them onto the back side of the fabric. Repeat this for all of your main fabric pieces.

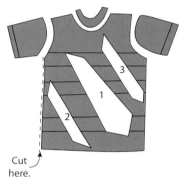

Cut here.

5. Cut 1 of each pattern piece from both fabrics, the main and the lining.

Sew

1. Using the main fabric, match up the raw edges of pieces 1 and 2 with right sides facing. Sew with a ¼″ seam allowance. The corners will hang off the edge some as shown; this is okay.

2. Sew pieces 2 and 3 together, repeating the process from Step 1. Then repeat Steps 1 and 2 with the lining pieces.

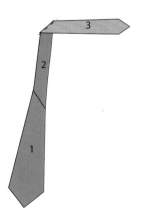

3. Pin the front and lining together with right sides together. Sew the top and bottom V's as shown with a ¼″ seam. Clip the points and turn right side out. Press. Topstitch these 2 seams if you like.

4. Baste the long edges with a ½″ seam. Finish the edges if you like with a zigzag or overlock stitch or with a serger.

Baste.

5. With the lining facing up, fold the left long side to the middle, aligning your basting stitch in the middle of the tie. Press.

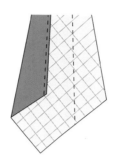

6. Using your finished edge or basting stitch as a guide, fold the right long side up ½″ and press.

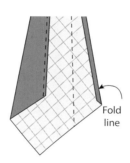

Fold line

7. Fold the right long side again, this time meeting the right side fold directly on top of the left long side in the middle of the necktie. Press.

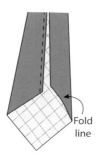

Fold line

8. Hand stitch the opening closed—a ladder stitch works well. (See Hand Stitches, page 17.)

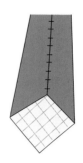

9. Press the finished tie.

Men's Necktie

POM-DOT SCARF

↱› YOU'LL NEED

1 extra large T-shirt

Bag of 1″ pom-poms

Embroidery floss (same/similar color as T-shirt)

Prep

1. Cut and remove the bottom half of the extra large T-shirt, cutting a straight line just below the armpit seams.

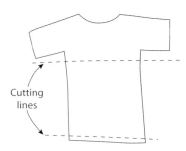

Cutting lines

2. Remove the bottom hem from T-shirt. You are left with 1 large tubular piece; this will become your scarf.

3. Cut straight from the bottom to the top, making a long rectangle.

NOTE: If you would like to make an infinity-style scarf, do not cut.

Instructions

1. Map out where you would like to place the pom-dots and mark each center spot with a water-soluble marking pen.

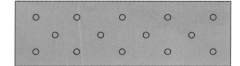

2. Take the 1″ pom-pom and place it on the underside of your scarf. Use the placement mark you made earlier to line up the dot.

3. Holding the pom-pom in place, tightly tie a length of embroidery floss on the top side to create the pom-dot. Finish the tie with a double knot and trim back excess threads.

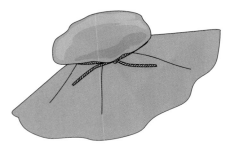

4. Repeat Steps 2 and 3 until you've covered all your marks.

5. Using scissors, cut a subtle scallop onto the short edges of your scarf. You could also choose to finish the scarf with a square edge, or to add fringe.

↱ > YOU'LL NEED

8 to 10 T-shirts in a variety of coordinating colors

A square quilt ruler (suggested 9½″) or create your own template from cardboard

Lightweight iron-on fusible interfacing—about 1 yard per 2 shirts

Poly/cotton blend batting—size based on the size of your quilt

Extra-wide backing or a flat sheet—try flannel for extra coziness

Safety pins—100 or so

Thread to match your backing fabric and a contrasting color

Crafter's paint in contrasting color

Sponge paintbrush

Blue painter's tape

Create with the heart;

build with the mind.

— Criss Jami —

Prepare

1. Choose your T-shirts! Make sure every shirt has been washed to prevent shrinking after the quilt is made.

2. If you want to use T-shirts with printed designs or logos in your quilt, place a square ruler over a T-shirt so that the design you want in your quilt is placed where you want it to be. A clear square will allow you to see the design through it, allowing for more accuracy. Remember that approximately ½″ around the edge of the square will not show after it is sewn.

Use your rotary cutter to cut around the ruler, leaving about 1″ of space around the ruler. Do this for all of your T-shirts. You are using the ruler as a rough guide at this point—after

you apply the interfacing in Step 4, the squares will be cut to the accurate size.

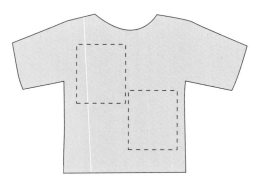

NOTE We chose to use T-shirt pieces with no printed designs on them; if you like this look but don't have enough plain shirts on hand, you can use the back of a printed shirt for a plain look.

3. Repeat Step 2 for all T-shirts.

4. Rough-cut the interfacing to match your T-shirt squares. Lay the cut squares on an ironing board with the right side

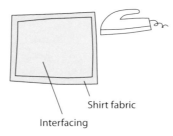

Shirt fabric

Interfacing

down. Place the interfacing rough side down so that it is against the shirt fabric. Iron on the interfacing, following the manufacturer's instructions. Avoid getting creases in the T-shirt fabric when you're ironing the interfacing.

5. Use a square ruler and rotary cutter to trim all of your interfaced squares to the same size. The size is up to you—if you started with a 9½″ square ruler, then trim your squares to that size.

6. Use a straight edge or larger ruler to cut your squares diagonally, creating 2 right triangles from each square.

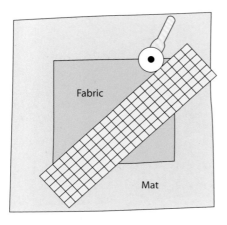

Fabric

Mat

7. Arrange your T-shirt triangles in a pattern pleasing to the eye. This can vary depending on how many triangles you have. Try to mix up lights and darks in a checker-

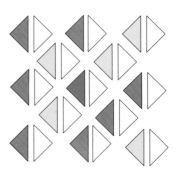

board pattern or get creative! There's no wrong way to lay out the quilt.

Sew

1. Put 2 triangles together face-to-face and sew together along the longest edge, using a ½″ seam allow-ance. Press the seams open. Continue with each square diagonally down the row.

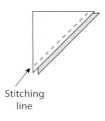

Stitching line

2. Sew the squares together into rows. Rows move diagonally in this quilt, so start from the top and move down and to the right with each square. Press the seam allowances down so that the row lies flat.

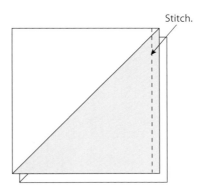

Stitch.

3. Beginning from the shortest row and the bottom left of your quilt, lay 1 row on top of another, right sides together. Start at the center seam and pin, trying to align the points where the angles meet as closely as possible. Sew the rows together using a ½″ seam allowance. Press the seams down so that the quilt front is as flat as possible.

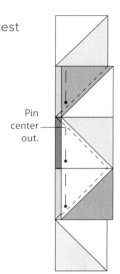

Pin center out.

4. Cut off the triangle halves at the top and bottom to create straight edges, and square up the corners of the quilt top.

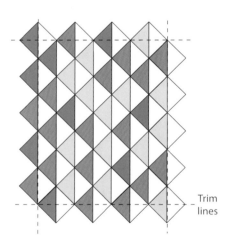

Trim lines

Paint

1. To add the painted accents, lay the quilt flat and use blue painter's tape to create stripes across the design.

2. Use your choice of contrasting crafter's paint and a sponge brush to apply a single solid layer of paint between the strips of tape. Let it dry.

Detail of painted lines

Finish

1. Lay down your choice of backing fabric, facedown, and keep it as flat as possible. Iron if needed. Use weights or books or painter's tape to keep each corner weighed down and held tight.

2. Lay out your batting on top of the fabric backing, ensuring that there are no creases or bumps.

3. Lay down your quilt front, faceup and centered on the batting. Pin the layers together using safety pins starting from the center of the quilt and moving outward. Pin at each seam intersection and along the edges.

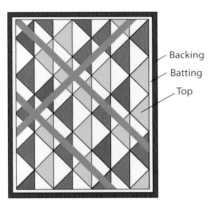

Backing
Batting
Top

4. Cut the batting so that it extends about 1˝ beyond the quilt front all the way around. Then trim the fabric backing so that it extends beyond the batting about 1½˝.

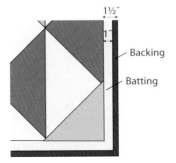

1½˝
1˝
Backing
Batting

5. Using your sewing machine with a bobbin thread matching your backing fabric and a contrasting thread on top, sew along the diagonal seams of your quilt about ¼˝ from the seam on either side. Start from the top, maintaining taut layers and removing pins as you approach them with your sewing machine needle. Proceed from the top to bottom, adding stitching along each diagonal seam.

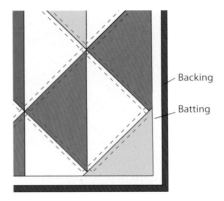

Backing
Batting

6. Lay the quilt flat. Fold the backing fabric over the batting.

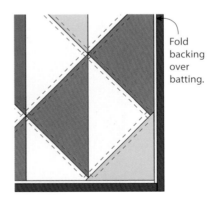

Fold backing over batting.

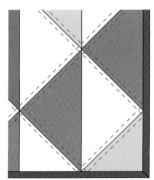

7. Create another fold in the backing fabric so that it creates a finished edge and pin onto the T-shirt quilt front. Do this all the way around the quilt. At the corners, you can either make a square turn, or make a diagonal cut so that it creates a mitered corner.

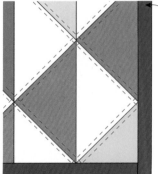

Fold backing and batting over to front of quilt.

Square corner

Trim corner and fold in.

Trim corner for miter and fold.

Mitered corner

8. Using a sewing machine, sew along the inside edge of the fabric border. For extra hold, you may also choose to sew along the outside edge of the quilt border.

tips > BACKING FABRIC

The options are endless for the back of your T-shirt quilt. To ensure that you get the correct amount of fabric, you may want to complete the first steps of the process so that you have the front of your quilt finished and you're able to measure it.

When choosing fabric, stick with fabrics that are easily washable and sturdy. You may choose to purchase your fabric from a fabric store or you could also use a flat sheet in the appropriate size. This is often the easier route because the sheets are wide enough to accommodate your quilt. Flannel is a favorite because it is warm, cozy, and durable and comes in a wide variety of colors and patterns. Fleece can be a good choice as well. It creates a much thicker and therefore much warmer quilt, but it can be slightly more difficult to manage in your sewing machine. Regardless of your fabric choice, pre-washing is a good idea.

> BATTING

You may or may not want to use batting. Batting will increase the warmth of the quilt and can make the quilt feel more substantial.

Batting comes in packages by size, or you may choose to buy it by the yard. Be sure to read the instructions on whether it requires pre-washing. Ideally, you want to find batting that is preshrunk. You don't want the batting to shrink after the quilt has been sewn together.

Another consideration is the manufacturer's recommendation for how close together the quilting lines need to be for the particular batting. This ranges from 4″ to 8″ or so; for this quilt you'll want to look for batting that doesn't require dense quilting. Or, you could choose to add more quilting lines.

ARM KNIT THROW

ARM KNIT THROW *I'm always up for a challenge and love learning new techniques. Hello, arm knitting. Quickly I embraced that the greatest thing about arm knitting is the lightning speed and fluid motions of making a chunky blanket. You won't need any background in knitting. However, if you have some experience, you're already ahead of the game. I'd like to introduce a couple terms before we get started.*

Tail—the yarn that goes from where you are working to the cut end of the yarn

Working yarn—the yarn that goes from where you are working to the balls of yarn

You can also find lots of videos demonstrating the arm-knitting technique on YouTube and elsewhere on the Internet.

→ YOU'LL NEED
660 yards T-shirt yarn

Your arms!

NOTE One large T-shirt provides about 13 yards of 2″-wide yarn. Different types of material content will stretch more or less. For this blanket I wanted to make sure that my yarn was bulky. The finished throw used 52 T-shirts that were cut into 2″-wide strips. If you'd like to use salvaged yardage (see Making Yardage, page 22) or new materials, you can cut approximately 22–25 yards of T-shirt yarn from 1 square yard of fabric (Making Yarn, page 24).

Prep

1. Take 2 balls or skeins of T-shirt yarn, place the 2 ends together, and treat it as if it were a single strand of thick yarn. For the sake of simplicity, the illustrations will show a single strand of yarn.

NOTE Make sure that your large balls of yarn will easily roll. I like to place the balls on the floor between my feet.

2. Measure 24 feet of yarn held double—this will be about 10–12 arm lengths. Now make a loop by taking the working yarn over the tail. Pull the working yarn through the loop and tighten to complete a slip knot. The slip knot should be loose enough that it can fit the widest part of your forearm.

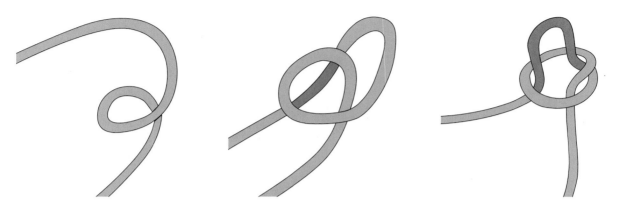

3. Place the slip knot on your right hand with the tail closer to you and the working yarn farther from you. You will be using the tail end to cast on your first row. From now on, the instructions will read as if there is just 1 strand for the working yarn and 1 for the tail—but you're actually working with double strands all the way through.

Casting On

1. With the slipknot loosely secured on your right wrist, let the 2 pieces of yarn dangle; put your forefinger and thumb between them.

2. Then spread your fingers apart, and at the same time, grab hold of both strands with your pinky finger. This forms a diamond shape with the yarn.

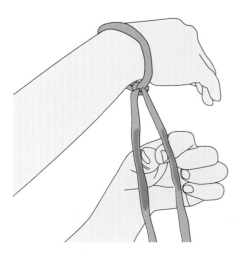

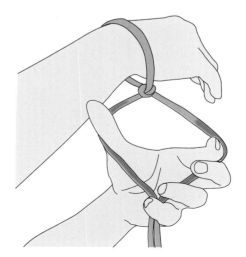

3. Now bring your right wrist down so the yarn forms a triangle/slingshot shape, with a loop over your left thumb and another loop over your left forefinger. This is the position for starting each stitch.

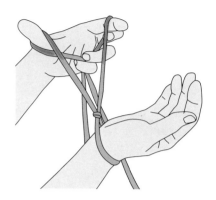

4. Using a couple fingers of your right hand, go under the loop on the front of your left thumb and pick up the working yarn that is looped around your left forefinger. Pull this through to form a new loop, and slip it over your right wrist.

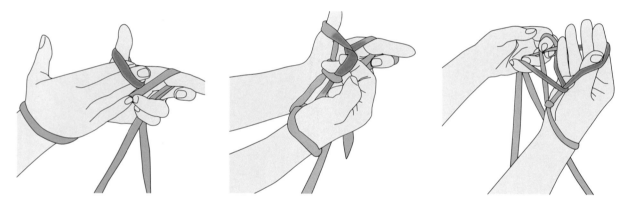

5. Pull the working yarn and tail apart to tighten the stitch on your arm. You'll want the stitches to be a bit snug on your arm, but not tight, as you continue to cast on. Push the stitches up your arm and onto your forearm. For the T-shirt throw, repeat Steps 1–4 to cast on 25 stitches.

Knitting

1. Pick up the working yarn and place it over the thumb on your right hand. (From now on, you will not need the tail yarn.) Close your fist over the working yarn. Pull the first stitch from your right arm over your fist.

tip >

The blanket will stitch up in less than an hour (not including prep time). If you find that the yarn becomes heavy on your arms or you need to take a break, simply complete the row you're working on, and then transfer all of the stitches one at a time onto the end of a broomstick.

Remember which arm you were working from; otherwise you might replace the blanket backward and your stitches will be reversed. The knit (smoother) side should be facing you. When you're ready to return to arm knitting, place the stitches from the broomstick to your arm and continue.

2. Pull the working yarn through the old stitch to make a new stitch, and place that on your left arm. After the old stitch is over your fist, drop it. Take the new stitch in your right fist, turn the loop a half turn, and place it on your left arm. You want the part of the loop that is in front of your hand (called the front leg of the stitch) to be the part that goes to the working yarn.

 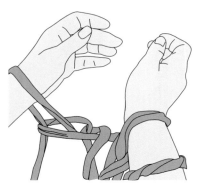

NOTE Keep your stitches as tight as possible for a full blanket...with smaller "holes."

3. Repeat to create 30 rows, knitting 1 row from your right arm to your left, and the next from your left arm to your right.

Binding Off

1. Start with all of your stitches on the same arm. (You can bind off from either arm.)

2. Knit 2 stitches onto your other arm. Take hold of the first stitch and pull it back over the second stitch and off your wrist.

3. Knit the next stitch onto your arm; you should again have 2 stitches. Again pick up the first stitch, pull it back over the second, and off your arm. As you continue to bind off, the stitches create a chain at the end of the blanket.

4. When you come to the end, you will have 1 remaining loop on your wrist. Take the loop off your arm and loosen it (make it bigger), so that the stitches won't pull out.

5. Pull 12″ or so from your working yarn roll and cut it, leaving it attached to your blanket. Take this short tail and bring it through the loop that remains. Pull the yarn end to tie off the last stitch, and then weave the end of the yarn into the stitches of the throw to secure it.

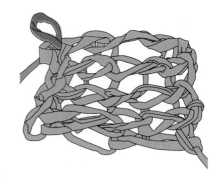

Seat Cushion

You can use smaller amounts of T-shirt yarn to knit comfy seat cushions for your chairs. It might take a little trial and error to find the right number of stitches to cast on, depending on the size of the chair, but these are so quick that you'll hardly notice!

To fit a standard seat, 18″–20″ wide and 16″–18″ deep, cast on 12 stitches with 10–12 knitted rows.

You need 61 yards or 182 feet of 2″–3″-wide yarn cut.

MACRAMÉ PLANT HANGER

With a series of strategically placed knots, you can create a lovely way to hang plants and complement your decor.

┌─> **YOU'LL NEED**

Wooden ring

4 strands of T-shirt yarn (page 24), twice the length you want your finished plant holder to be

Ceiling hook

1. Thread the 4 strands of yarn evenly through the wooden ring and secure with a knot. This is going to be the tippy top of your macramé plant hanger. Now you'll have 8 strands of yarn to work with.

2. Separate the 8 strands into 4 pairs.

3. Measure down to the point where you want your plant in a pot to hang, and knot the yarn pairs there.

4. Knot each strand with a partner from the neighboring pair. Don't forget to knot the furthest left and right strands together too; you are essentially creating a ring of knots.

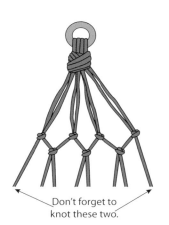

Don't forget to knot these two.

5. Repeat Step 4.

6. To finish, knot all the ends together, and trim them to the desired length.

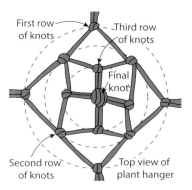

First row of knots

Third row of knots

Final knot

Second row of knots

Top view of plant hanger

7. Insert your potted plant into this string network, and hang from a hook in the ceiling.

CIRCLE PILLOW

↱➤ YOU'LL NEED

Burlap—a square a few inches bigger than your finished pillow

T-shirt yarn—for a 12˝ circle, about 40 yards of yarn made from 1˝ strips

Permanent marker

Crochet hook size 4.25mm or G

Needle and thread

T-shirt fabric—a piece 2˝ larger than your finished pillow size

Pillow form in your desired pillow size, or polyfill or fabric scraps

Prep

1. For a 12˝ × 12˝ pillow, cut a 16˝ × 16˝ square from burlap. Mark a 12˝ circle in the center.

2. Using a permanent marker, draw your design onto burlap. (I drew several concentric circles for my design.) Then cut out a circle, leaving 2˝ around the outer edge of your design.

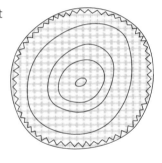

3. Zigzag or straight stitch ½˝ from the edge. This will keep the burlap from unraveling while you work.

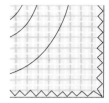

4. Cut T-shirt yarn 1˝ wide. (See Making Yarn, page 24.)

5. Use a crochet hook to pull an end of the T-shirt yarn from the bottom of the burlap through the top.

6. Put your crochet hook through a hole in the burlap near where you pulled up the first bit of yarn, and hook a loop of T-shirt yarn. Pull the yarn through to the top to form a bump (or "kernel") on the top side. Continue to pull more kernels to the top.

Follow your pattern, changing colors as needed, until the pillow top is covered with kernels. Leave a border of plain burlap at least 1˝ around your finished design.

7. When you're finished with a color, snip the end of the yarn flush with the rest of the kernels.

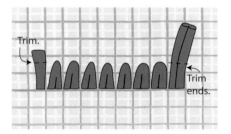

8. Trim the fabric for the back of the pillow to match the size of your finished pillow top. Pin the back to the top, right sides together. Stitch them together, leaving an opening big enough to stuff the pillow form in (you can compress the pillow form quite a bit!), or big enough for your hand if you're using other filling.

9. Turn the pillow right side out and stuff it. Pin the open edges and hand stitch using a simple whipstitch (page 17).

Use this technique to create a pillow any size and shape you'd like. Just create a pattern and mark it on burlap.

DEER PLUSHIES *This stuffed buck and stuffed doe are so cute that they might find a home on your bed instead of in the kids' toy chest.*

⌐> YOU'LL NEED

(For one toy)

3 T-shirts or large scraps from other projects

6 oz. of polyfill

½ cup of rice

Wooden dowel or blunt tool for turning

Iron

½ yard lightweight interfacing

¼ yard fusible webbing *(optional)*

Walking foot *(optional)*

Thread

Never tell people how to do things. Tell them what to do and they will surprise you with their ingenuity.

— George S. Patton —

Prep

1. Using the patterns (pages 74–77), create templates.

2. Cut:

15″ × 15″ rectangle of brown and interfacing for head, ears, arms, and legs

7″ × 8″ square of beige and interfacing for antlers

6″ × 12″ square of your choice and interfacing for shirt

NOTE: Additional materials are needed for the cape.

3. Iron interfacing to the back of T-shirt material. Use templates and a water-soluble marker to trace your 4 pieces each for antlers and ears, and 2 pieces each for the head, shirt/body, arms, and legs.

4. Cut out the pieces you've marked on interfaced fabric.

5. Trace the eye and nose patterns onto scrap fabric. You may choose to fuse them to the head before stitching them—in this case, apply a piece of fusible web to the wrong side of the fabric scraps before cutting out the eye and nose patterns.

Assemble

1. Pin the nose and eyes to the head piece; now is the time to fuse them if you chose to use webbing. Then appliqué them by topstitching around the edge of each piece.

Repeat the same process for any embellishments on the shirt including necktie, superhero, and so forth.

2. Match up the front head piece to the front body/shirt piece at neckline with right sides facing together. Pin in place. Sew together using a ¼″ seam. Repeat for the back pieces.

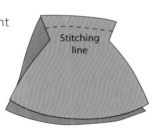

Stitching line

3. Fold the 2 arm rectangles and 2 leg rectangles in half lengthwise with right sides together. Press and pin to hold in place. Begin your stitch in the middle of a short side, stitch forward ½″, and then backstitch to edge. Going forward again, continue sewing with a ¼″ seam allowance across the bottom and up the long side. Backstitch again when you reach the top. Repeat with remaining limbs.

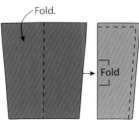

Fold.

Fold

4. Use a blunt object (like an eraser end of a pencil) to help you turn the arm/leg tube right side out. Fill with polyfill until the arms and legs are stiff. Leave ½″ empty at open end.

5. Carefully line up the antlers, right sides together, and pin to hold them in place. Stitch from a bottom edge, all the way around to the other bottom edge, leaving the bottom open. Backstitch at each end of the seam.

tip >

For delicate maneuvering, set your sewing machine to position your needle down when stopped. Sew slowly, and when you come to a curve, stop. Lift up your presser foot (your needle position should be down and holding the fabric in place), gently turn fabric, set presser foot down, and continue sewing. This is a great trick to keep your stitches consistent around corner edges without puckering as well.

6. Clip the sharp corners and notch the curves, being careful not to cut into the seam. Turn

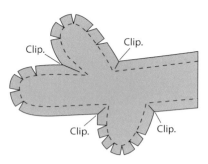

Clip.

Clip.

Clip.

Clip.

the antlers right side out and stuff with poly-fill, leaving ½″ empty at the open end.

7. Sew the ear triangles together, leaving straight end open. Turn right side out.

8. Lay out the front deer body with right side facing up. We're going to make a burrito of sorts! Arrange your stuffed arms, legs, antlers, and unstuffed ears and pin them in place.

You will want to leave a little bit of the head free on the outside edge of your ears so that there is room for a seam around the head.

9. Place back of deer body right side facing down and repin arms, legs, ears, and antlers into place through all the layers. It will be a bulging pocket of goodness.

10. Start sewing around the outside edge of your deer between the antlers with a ¼″ seam; be sure to secure your seam by back-stitching at the beginning and

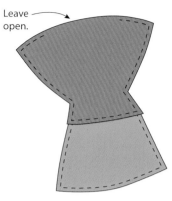

Leave open.

end. Leave an opening approximately 3″ between the antlers to turn it.

11. Turn the deer right side out. Fill first with ½ cup of rice to weight the bottom, then fill with polyfill until firm. Fold the open edges in and pin closed.

12. Using a sharp needle and thread that matches the section you're sewing (brown), use an invisible ladder stitch (see Hand Stitches, page 17) to finish off the deer.

Optional Costumes

You can use T-shirt scraps to make costumes for your deer (see Applique, page 19).

For the cape, trace the template onto any knit scrap or jersey knit material. Cut out the cape and attach it by tying it around the neck of your deer plushie.

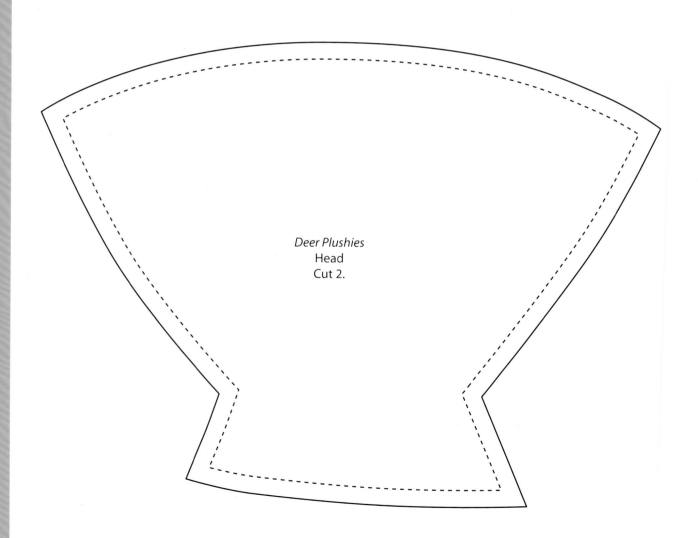

Fold

Deer Plushies
Arm
Cut 2 on fold.

Deer Plushies
Head
Cut 2.

┌─────── Fold ───────┐

Deer Plushies
Leg
Cut 2 on fold.

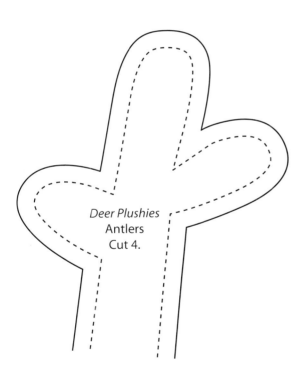

Deer Plushies
Antlers
Cut 4.

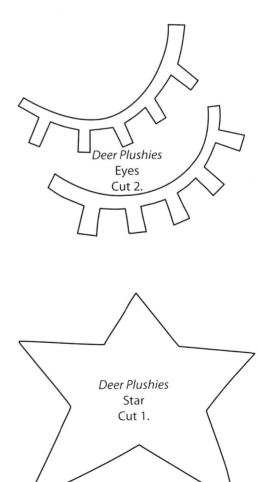

Deer Plushies
Eyes
Cut 2.

Deer Plushies
Star
Cut 1.

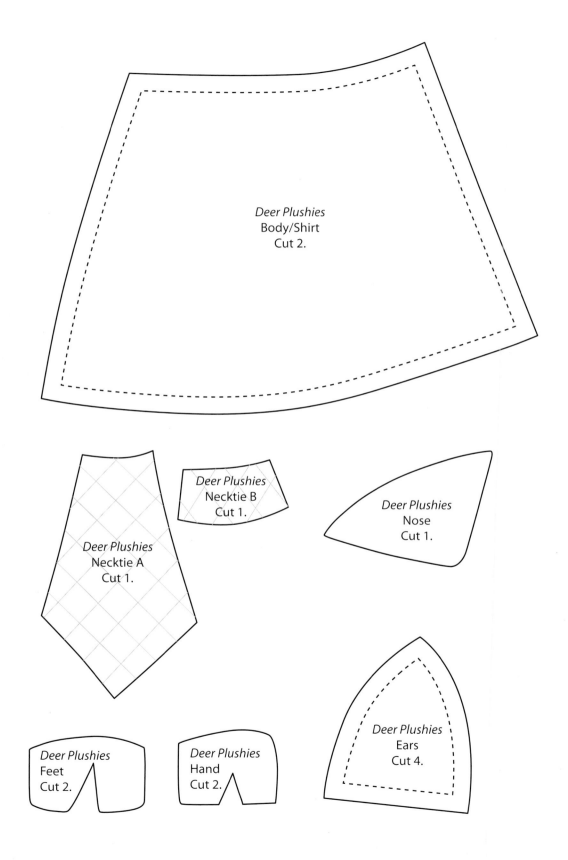

Deer Plushies
Body/Shirt
Cut 2.

Deer Plushies
Necktie B
Cut 1.

Deer Plushies
Nose
Cut 1.

Deer Plushies
Necktie A
Cut 1.

Deer Plushies
Feet
Cut 2.

Deer Plushies
Hand
Cut 2.

Deer Plushies
Ears
Cut 4.

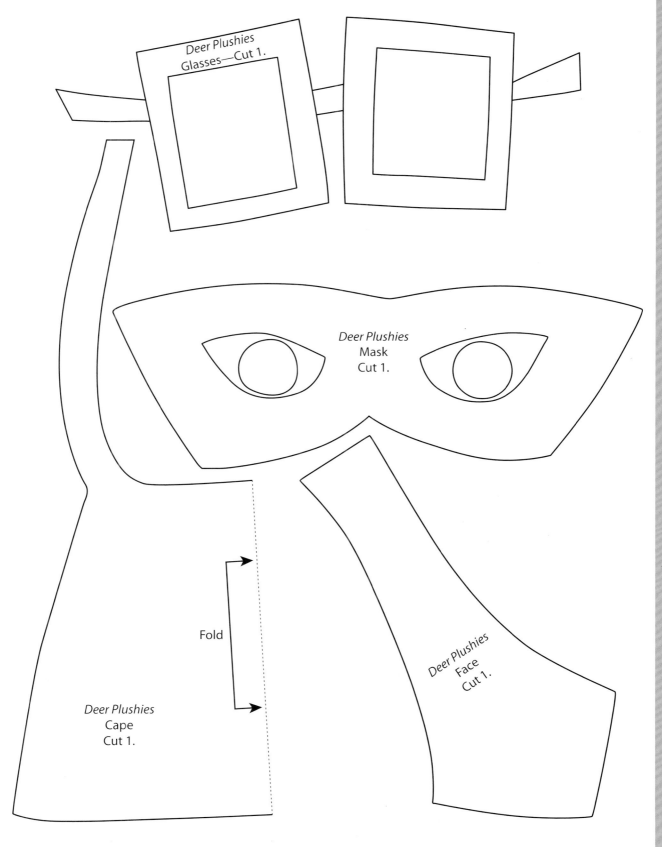

Deer Plushies
Glasses—Cut 1.

Deer Plushies
Mask
Cut 1.

Fold

Deer Plushies
Cape
Cut 1.

Deer Plushies
Face
Cut 1.

KID'S ART SMOCK *Messes are a wonderful thing—until you realize that your wall has been freshly repainted with a swirly mix of golds, greens, and browns that now trails across your house. If there is one thing I love about creating with (and for) kids, it's that their minds are open to seeing things differently. You see a wall; they see a blank canvas. Whether you're getting hands-on with science experiments or crafting up the latest creations in your home or classroom, your little artist will love this personalized art smock. It might save their clothes; it won't save your walls.*

▸ YOU'LL NEED

2 large kids T-shirts (anything larger than sizes 4–6)

Needle and thread

tip ❭

You can customize the fit of the smock by using another T-shirt as a template. The pattern provided best fits kids who are 2 to 4 years old.

Prep

1. Begin by laying your main T-shirt out on the table. Fold in half lengthwise.

2. Using the pattern provided (pullout page P1), trace and cut out the body of your smock. Match up the pattern to the shoulder seams and the center front/back of the T-shirt. Keep the original shoulders and neck of the T-shirt intact.

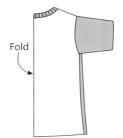

Fold

3. Hem the arm openings for a more finished look. Fold in ¼˝ and press flat. Stitch ⅛˝ from fold with a zigzag stitch.

NOTE If you're in a hurry, you can skip this step and leave the raw edges. Remember, T-shirt knit will not fray!

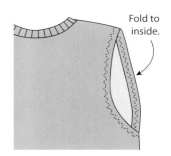

Fold to inside.

4. Take the bottom hem from the second T-shirt to make your pocket; the hemmed edge will be the top of the pocket. Cut a strip as wide as the front of the smock and about 6″ high.

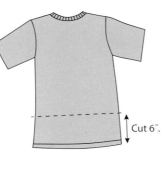

Cut 6″.

Before attaching it to your smock, mark placement for pocket divisions with a marking tool. Then line up bottom edge of pocket with bottom of the smock and pin into place along the top.

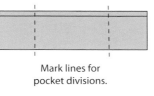

Mark lines for pocket divisions.

5. Sew directly on top of the marks for pocket divisions, from top to bottom, backstitching at the top.

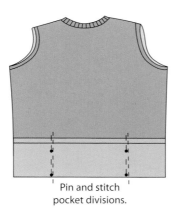

Pin and stitch pocket divisions.

6. Turn the shirt inside out. Pin at the sides and then sew with a ¼″ seam allowance. Sew from armhole down each side to bottom of smock, catching the sides of the pocket in the seams.

7. To hem the bottom, fold up ¼″, iron, fold up another ¼″, and iron again. Turn right side out and sew hem in place.

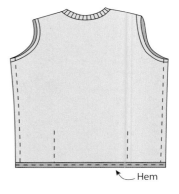

Hem

Kid's Art Smock

CUFF BRACELETS

CUFF BRACELETS *Sweat bands, superhero cuffs, or staple fashion accessories—these cuff bracelets are fun for the whole family!*

> YOU'LL NEED

2 T-shirt sleeves

Lightweight fusible interfacing

Needle and thread

Prep

You can use 2 sleeves left over from a previous T-shirt project. Cut along the underarm seam and press flat. Layering 1 sleeve on top of the other, cut out a long rectangle that measures 6″ × 2½″.

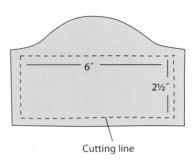

Cutting line

Sewing Instructions

1. Customize your desired design onto the center of the cuff.

tip > YOUR DESIGNS

Some pattern choices have been provided for you (page 85). You can use them to create appliqué pieces for your cuffs. You can create your own designs as well. Also, you can cut out and reuse a graphic from a screen-printed T-shirt. Cuffs can be customized with fabric paint, markers, or embroidery (page 18).

2. Set your sewing machine to make your stitches just a bit longer than you use for everyday sewing, then sew the 2 layers together along the long edges.

Sew cuff.

3. Fold the right sides together, matching the short ends. Sew a seam along the short ends with a ¼˝ seam allowance, back-stitching at each end, and reinforce with a zigzag stitch.

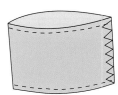

Stitch short ends together.

ABCDEF
GHIJKL
MNOPQ
RSTUV
WXYZ

Cuff Bracelets

PET TOYS *Have you ever brought home a squeaky new toy for that lovable fur ball of yours, only to be met with uninterest—or worse yet, to see it torn to pieces in minutes? The cost of dog toys can add up quickly. Why not make your own? By using up those worn out T-shirts, you're not only reducing waste, helping to protect the environment (and your favorite armchair), but also giving your pet a toy that already has a familiar and friendly smell. These tugs are so easy to make that you can even stash a few away for another day. Be careful where you stash a catnip toy. The kitties will seek them out!*

Dog Tug

NOTE
This makes a toy for a large dog. For smaller dogs you can use shorter lengths of yarn and fewer pieces.

⌐> YOU'LL NEED
20 lengths 1″ × 20″ of T-shirt yarn in a variety of colors (See Making Yarn, page 24.)

Assemble

Lay your pieces together in 2 sets of 10. Twist each set separately.

Then twist the 2 sections together and tie a large knot at each end. Your knot should be tight and secure.

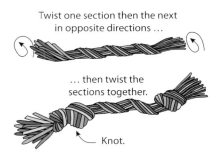

Twist one section then the next in opposite directions …

… then twist the sections together.

Knot.

Catnip Knots

⌐> YOU'LL NEED
Quality catnip • Large T-shirt scraps

Prep

1. Cut 4″ × 7″ rectangles from scraps. The shape or size doesn't have to be exact, but make sure you have enough room to secure your catnip in a knot.

2. Place 1 teaspoon of catnip in the center of fabric pieces.

Add catnip to center. 1 tsp.

3. Take 1 rectangle and start at the long edge near you, tightly rolling the catnip in the material to create a tube. Tie the tube into a knot, securing your catnip inside.

Roll.

4. Cut edges to create fringe.

Tie knot and fringe.

REVERSIBLE DOG SHIRT

REVERSIBLE DOG SHIRT *This shirt is for a small dog. They tend to be more appreciative of shirts than larger dogs are. But photocopying the pattern at a zillion percent (or 500% maybe) might get you a shirt that will fit your big dog. But you're on your own trying to wrestle him into it!*

‣> YOU'LL NEED

2 large T-shirts for small- to medium-sized dog

Needle and thread

Hook-and-loop tape (such as Velcro)

Pattern piece: Reversible Dog Shirt (pullout page P2)

1. Start by removing the sleeves and neckline from your T-shirts (see Deconstructing a T-Shirt, page 10). The first T-shirt will be the front and the second will be the lining. Cut each shirt down the center back from neckline to hemline.

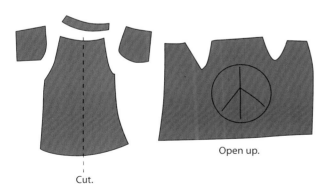

Cut.

2. Fold a shirt in half, centering the graphic on the front of the T-shirt.

3. Match the fold line on the pattern piece to the center fold of the shirt. Trace and cut out the pattern piece.

Open up.

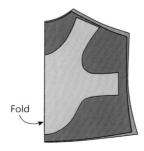

Fold

4. Repeat Steps 2 and 3 for your lining T-shirt as well.

5. Open your cut pieces, line up the edges, and pin them right sides together. Sew the layers together using a ¼˝ seam allowance, and remember to leave a 3˝ opening to turn. For tips, see Sewing with Knits (page 20).

Leave open.

6. Clip along the curved areas and trim away corners. Then turn right side out through the opening.

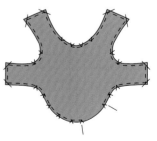

7. Press the seams, turning the open edges to the inside, and finish with a topstitch near the edge all the way around.

8. Place the hook tape on the outer T-shirt and the loop on the inside fabric. Refer to the pattern or image for placement.

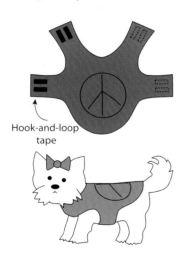

Hook-and-loop tape

9. Stitch the tape into place, sewing about ⅛˝ from each edge.

To: Eva
From: Alicia

GIFT BOWS *This is a quick way to use up some T-shirts to great effect!*

> **YOU'LL NEED:**
T-shirt

Glue gun

Needle and thread
(*hand stitching optional*)

Felt (*optional*)

The purpose of life is not to be happy. It is to be useful, to be honorable, to be compassionate, to have it make some difference that you have lived and lived well.

— Ralph Waldo Emerson —

Prep

1. Square up your fabric and cut (using rotary cutter, ruler, and cutting mat) 3″-wide strips. You will have approximately 4 large loops, and this will make 4 gift bows.

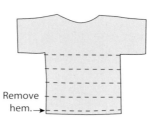

Remove hem. →

2. Take 1 loop and cut to make a long strip.

3. Fold the strip in half lengthwise, and make 1″ cuts along the length

Hot glue inside.

Fold.

Cut.

of the fabric about ½″ apart—you're cutting through the folded edge and leaving about ½″ uncut along the raw edges. (Pssst! I use scissors here, and generally don't measure.)

4. Hot glue along the edge and roll as you go, continuing to add glue.

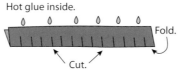

Roll.

5. When you're finished you should have a pouf.

6. Finish it off by covering the bottom with felt and either gluing or hand sewing to secure it.

tip >

I add a pin to the back; that way the gift topper can easily be repurposed as a brooch or a flower embellishment for a headband or hat. It's an added gift!

POM-POMS *These are just adorable and easy to make—no sewing! And you can find many uses for them. Pom-poms are great as decor. Make a bunch of mini-poms, and with the help of a hot glue gun, create a fun wreath. String them as garland. Or double the length of the smaller strip and your pom can be used to tie gift bags or packages for anyone.*

❯ YOU'LL NEED

T-shirt yarn

2 empty cardboard
toilet paper rolls

1. Using Method 1: Making Yarn (page 24), cut 10–15 strips 1˝ wide.

2. Cut a 4˝ piece for tying the pom-pom together.

3. Hold 2 empty toilet paper rolls together sideways and wrap the T-shirt yarn around the outside. When you get to the end of a T-shirt strip, hold it in place with your thumb and start a new strip. Make sure the new strip overlaps the end of the old one. Repeat with all strips.

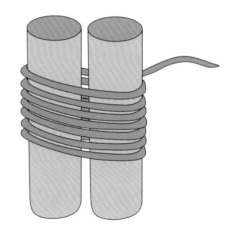

4. Take the 4˝ piece of T-shirt yarn and slide it between the toilet paper rolls. Tie a tight knot around the wound T-shirt yarn.

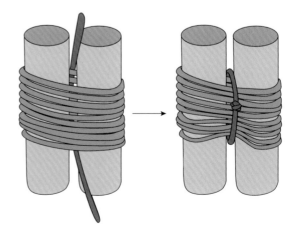

5. With sharp scissors, carefully cut each loop along each side of the tissue roll. Fluff up the pom-pom.

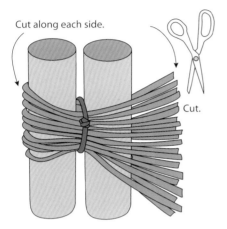

Cut along each side.

Cut.

Tip to Save the Planet

Recycle your cardboard! It uses less energy, water, and oil to recycle cardboard than it does to create new cardboard. Recycling and reusing saves space in landfills. And it's better for the environment because less chemical waste and methane gas are produced.

HOLIDAY STOCKING *Deck the halls with your favorite T-shirts!*

Santa promises not to stuff your upcycled stocking with coal this year.

> YOU'LL NEED

2 T-shirts

Scraps

1 flannel shirt (*optional—you can use recycled flannel for the lining of the stocking instead of a second T-shirt*)

Fusible webbing

Thread

Prep

Cut out all pattern shapes (see Holiday Stocking Pattern, pullout page P1) from T-shirts. Cut through both the front and back layer of a T-shirt for 2 toe panels (1 in each direction), 2 outer pieces, 2 lining pieces, 2 heels, and toe appliqué pieces.

Sew

1. Using fusible webbing if you choose to, use the appliqué technique (see How to Appliqué, page 19) to attach the toe and heel to the front panel.

2. Pair 1 lining and 1 outside piece, right sides together. Be sure that the toes are facing the same direction. Sew ¼˝ along top edge. Open and press seam. Repeat this step with the other outside and lining pieces.

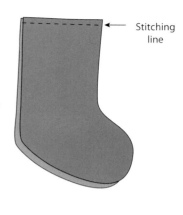

Stitching line

3. Line up both of your units from Step 2 with right sides together. Match the seam you just sewed and pin the units together. Sew around the entire piece with a ¼˝ seam allowance, leaving 3˝ open in the lining to turn.

4. Cut notches into the outside fabric, especially around the toe. (This helps the fabric to sit nicely and not pucker.) Be careful not to snip through your seam. On your lining side, trim close to seam to reduce bulk.

5. Turn the stocking right side out through opening. Fold in the open edges. Pin; then topstitch closed with coordinating thread.

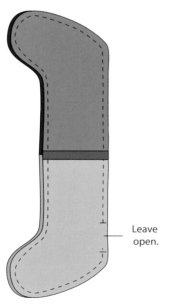

Leave open.

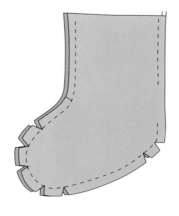

Stitch.

6. Tuck the lining inside. (*Optional:* Topstitch around the outside edge near the seamline.)

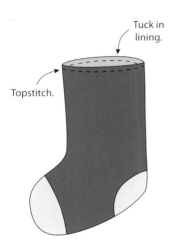

Tuck in lining.

Topstitch.

7. Add hanging tab by cutting 2 layers of T-shirt materials and attach with topstitching all the way around.

CHRISTMAS TREE SKIRT

CHRISTMAS TREE SKIRT *Create a darling, casual, and any-color-you-want tree skirt. With the layers and fringe, this one has a light, airy, and bouncy look.*

↱❯ YOU'LL NEED

12 T-shirts

1½ yards of quality felt

Measuring tape

Needle and thread

Marking pen

Coordinating thread

Tip to Save the Planet
Use an old tree skirt as the base for this new skirt (instead of purchasing felt). After all, we love to reuse!

Make the Skirt Base

1. Fold your felt in half and then fold it again to create 4 rectangles.

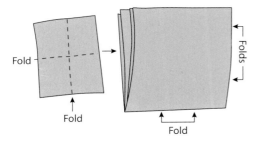

2. Use the measuring tape to mark your fabric from 1 side across to the other at 24″. From the point where your folded edges meet, use a

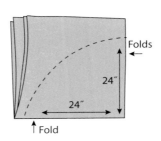

safety pin to hold your measuring tape in place. Using it like a compass, mark 24″ to create a semicircle.

3. Cut out the semicircle. When you unfold it, you will have a standard size (48″) tree skirt. But don't unfold it yet!

4. Create the center hole for the tree base. Measure from folded edge to 3″ and mark a half circle, as in Step 2. Cut along your lines.

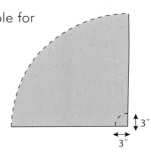

Make the Fringe

1. Cut a T-shirt horizontally just below the armpit and again above the hem. Then cut again horizontally in half. You should now have 2 continuous loops, approximately 7″ wide. Cut each loop to have a length of fabric.

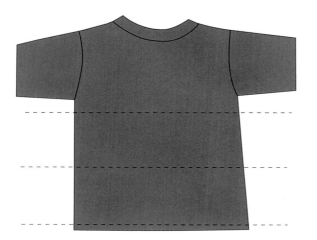

2. Repeat Step 1 for the rest of the T-shirts.

NOTE Keep in mind that different shirts will yield a different amount or size of fabric. We are not working with exact math. If you need additional fabric, cut material from the scraps of shirts and sleeves in your bins.

3. Unfold the base of the tree skirt. Lay 1 length of fabric 4″ from the outside edge of the base; pin to hold in place. It's better to have too many pins than not enough pins. Continue adding your strips along the edge, overlapping when new pieces are added.

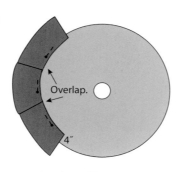

Overlap.

4″

tip > CURVES

Do not pull or force the fabric around the curves, but let it rest lightly. I found it was easier to use smaller chunks of the shirt, overlapping them all the way around the skirt. Or you could lay the T-shirt down and pleat it to conform to the circle shape.

4. Sew your first layer into place using a straight stitch. If you have a walking foot, this is a perfect project to use it on. Don't forget to backstitch at the beginning and end.

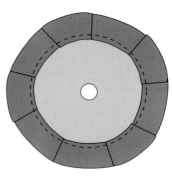

5. Start laying out your next strips of fabric in a layer 3″ above the first one. Repeat Step 4.

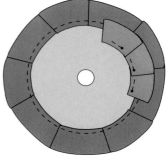

6. Repeat Step 5 until you've filled the entire skirt with T-shirt fabric strips.

7. To cut the fringe, begin with the outside row. Fold the other rows up and out of the way as you're cutting. The example pictured has strips cut about 1″ wide, but it varied. Use sharp scissors and stop cutting just below the stitch line. Cut each row at a time until you're finished.

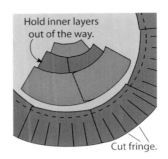

Hold inner layers out of the way.

Cut fringe.

8. Use a rotary cutter and straight edge to cut an opening from the outside edge to the inside circle. This will allow you to slip the tree skirt around the tree base.

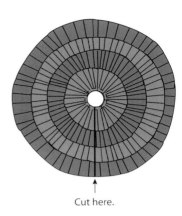

Cut here.

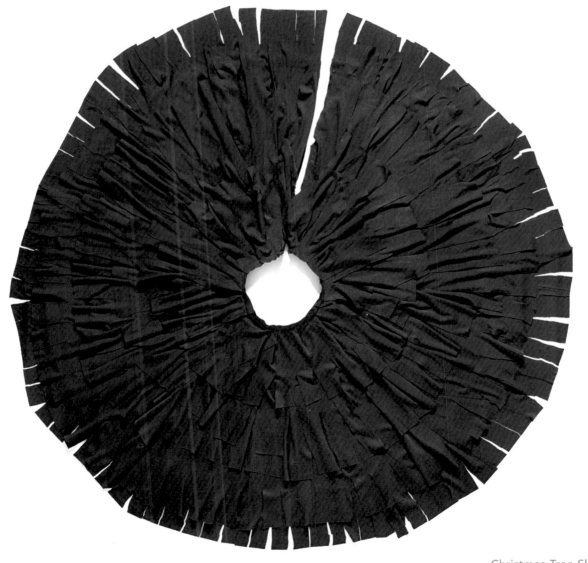

RUFFLE GLOBE PARTY BALLS *Color-coordinate these with your party theme and add a pop to the setting. You know … there is no reason they have to come down. They add some cheer to your house, porch, or patio.*

Prep

1. With your T-shirt spread out on the cutting mat, remove the bottom hem.

2. Fold the T-shirt in half lengthwise. Starting at the bottom of the shirt, measure and cut 3″ widths using a rotary cutter and straight edge.

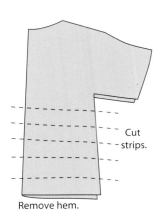

Cut strips.

Remove hem.

3. Repeat this process until you come just below the armpit seams.

4. Cut the loops created in Steps 2 and 3 at both ends, making 2 strips of equal length.

5. Create ruffles with the T-shirt strips.

Ruffles

By Hand

1. Using a ballpoint needle with knotted thread, sew a straight stitch (sometimes called a basting stitch or running stitch; see Hand Stitches, page 17) 1″ from the bottom of the strip until you reach the other end of the fabric. This will keep the gathers bunched tightly toward the bottom and loosely at the top.

NOTE Your hand sewing doesn't have to be anywhere near perfect. These stitches will not be seen after we glue them into place.

tip ⟩

Your stitch length determines how big the ruffles will be. Use long, gapped stitches for widely spaced ruffles or short stitches for close-together ruffles. I run my stitches about ¼″ apart.

2. Hold the thread tail while pulling fabric toward the original knot (at the first stitch) to create ruffles.

3. Space the ruffles as you wish and tie off the long end of thread with a knot and trim the thread.

By Machine

1. Before beginning, change out your bobbin thread so that it *doesn't* match your top thread or your T-shirt material.

2. Lengthen your stitch length to the longest setting available. If you're unsure of how to do this, please check your machine manual for instructions. Sew a straight stitch 1″ from the bottom of the strip to the other end of the fabric. When you reach the end of the strip, stop, lift the presser foot, and keep 2″–3″ of tail thread on the end.

3. Pull *only* the bobbin thread and push fabric down the thread to create a ruffle. When finished, tie off with a secure knot.

Rosettes

1. Create rosettes with the ruffled strip by coiling the bottom edge (where stitched), adding dots of glue as you go to keep fabric coiled.

Roll up the ruffle while dotting with hot glue.

2. Use hot glue to secure each rosette to the Styrofoam ball. Two extra large T-shirts are enough to completely cover a 6″ ball. If you have uneven ends of ruffles sticking up, trim them now.

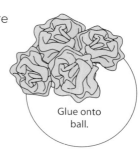

Glue onto ball.

Finish

Use a strip of coordinating ribbon pinned into the top of your ball for hanging.

NO LONGER DISPOSABLE

Do your little bit of good where you are. It's those little bits of good put together that overwhelm the world.

— Desmond Tutu —

I don't recall being taught to recycle or reuse. My first introduction to the concept was sometime in elementary school when as first graders we would collect paper for recycling throughout the school. It was one of those privileges you were given to leave the classroom with a buddy … unsupervised by the teachers! Even then I didn't actually understand what it all meant.

My commitment to reuse before recycling is something that is practiced daily in my home. It's my hope for my children, your family, and future generations alike that we're able to instill the values and ideas now so that it's not a habit that needs to be learned—it becomes their way of life.

I've included simple and fun ways to practice in your everyday lives and create a happy and healthy home in this last section of projects.

UNPAPER TOWELS

UNPAPER TOWELS *Before paper towels, there were cloth napkins, which worked great at wiping spills and chins. And they still do. Cloth napkins often seem like a luxury these days, but these are the "unpaper" towel, meant to be used any time.*

Tip to Save the Planet

One-third of garbage that enters our landfills is paper products. Eliminating paper towels from your daily habit for one month will reduce your carbon footprint by 5.8 pounds and save you approximately $8.

▸ YOU'LL NEED

Makes 1 Unpaper Towel.

1 T-shirt • Marker/chalk

Prep

1. Turn your T-shirt inside out and lay it flat.

2. Draw a rectangle on the T-shirt. Start by marking a line just below the collar of the T-shirt using your straight edge and washable marker. Draw 2 parallel lines down the sides of the shirt close to the sleeve stitching. Finish the rectangle with a line near the bottom hem.

3. Pin around the inside of the rectangle. Be sure to go through both layers of the shirt. Cut out along the lines.

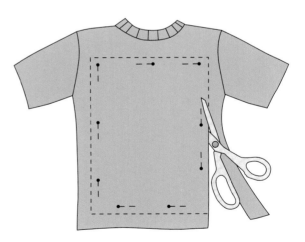

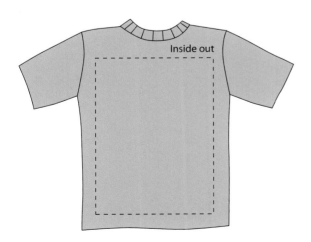

Sew

1. Sew along the outside edge using a ¼˝ seam allowance. Leave a 3˝ opening along the side to turn the unpaper towel right side out. (See Sewing with Knits, page 20.)

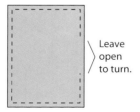

Leave
open
to turn.

2. Trim the corners at an angle.

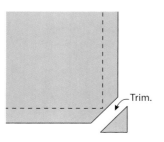

Trim.

3. Carefully turn the towel right side out through the 3˝ opening. Push out your corners. Iron to press edge seams flat, turning the edges of your opening to the inside.

4. Pin the opening closed, and then pin around the edges.

5. Topstitch around the outside of your reusable napkin about ⅛˝ from the edge.

REUSABLE DUSTER MITT

REUSABLE DUSTER MITT *Let's face it; no one really wants to dust, do they? But there's something satisfying about removing dust with repurposed material. Instead of meeting the landfill, it now serves a noble purpose, thanks to your creativity!*

YOU'LL NEED

2 contrasting T-shirts*

1 sleeve cuff from long-sleeved shirt

* One T-shirt will yield enough fabric for this project, but contrasting colors add a fun pop.

Prep

1. Cut a 10″ × 5″ rectangle along the fold at 1 side of your main T-shirt; keep the shirt's hem along 1 of the 5″ sides of the rectangle. When you unfold it, the piece will measure 10″ × 10″. Set aside.

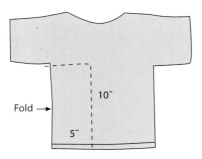

Fold →   10″   5″

2. Cut at least 8 strips, 4 from each T-shirt, approximately 10″ × 3″.

3. Cut about 1″ in and 1½″ apart along both long edges of each strip to create a fringe.

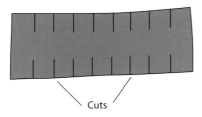

Cuts

4. Open up the 10″ × 5″ rectangle from Step 1 and smooth it out.

Sew

1. Stack a fringe of each color, lengthwise, 2″ from right edge of rectangle. Pin in place. Run a single length of stitches in coordinating thread down the center of fringe, backstitching at each end.

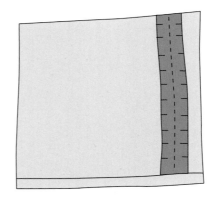

2. Repeat Step 1 for the remaining fringed strips, spacing each approximately 2″ apart. Note: I found it easier to sew 1 set of strips and then fold over the fringe before laying out the next set.

3. With the fringe sewn in place, fold the rectangle in half, right sides in, with the fringe running vertically. Pin into place, being careful not to catch any of the fringe. Leave an opening on the short side with the original shirt hem; this will serve as the bottom of your mitt.

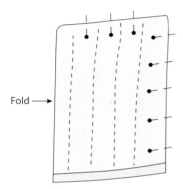

Fold →

4. Draw a rounded shape on the top of the mitt and re-pin around the edges. Sew or serge the edges and trim the seam allowance. Turn your mitt right side out.

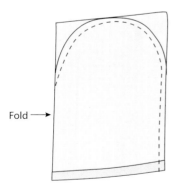

Fold →

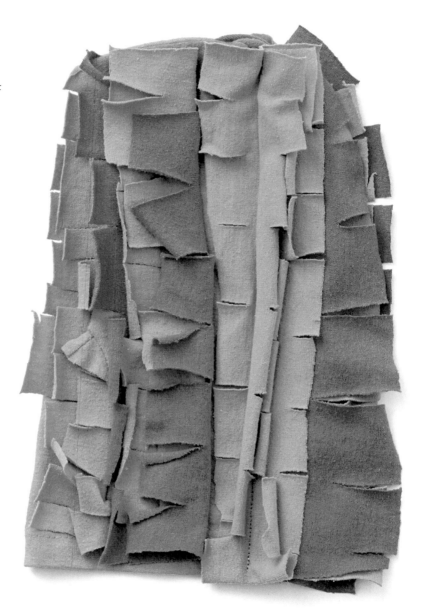

Dust Mop Refills

2. Cut 10″ × 3″ T-shirt strips from the rest of the rectangle to create ruffles—3 to 5 strips will work. (See Ruffle Globe Party Balls, page 104, for making ruffles.)

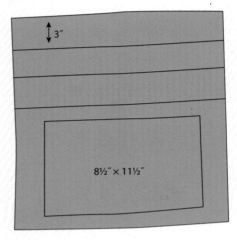

3″

8½″ × 11½″

3. Sew ruffles lengthwise onto the center 5″ of the 8½″ × 11½″ rectangle from Step 1. Now your cloth is ready to wrap around the duster and poke into the holes on top—just like the nonrecyclable paper it's replacing.

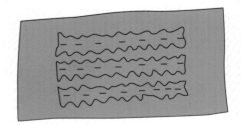

Do you love your moplike duster-on-a-stick? You can make reusable cloths for it following the instructions for the Unpaper Towel (page 108), with a few small adjustments.

1. Cut a large T-shirt rectangle, following Step 1 of Unpaper Towel (page 108). Cut 1 rectangle 8½″ × 11½″ from the larger rectangle.

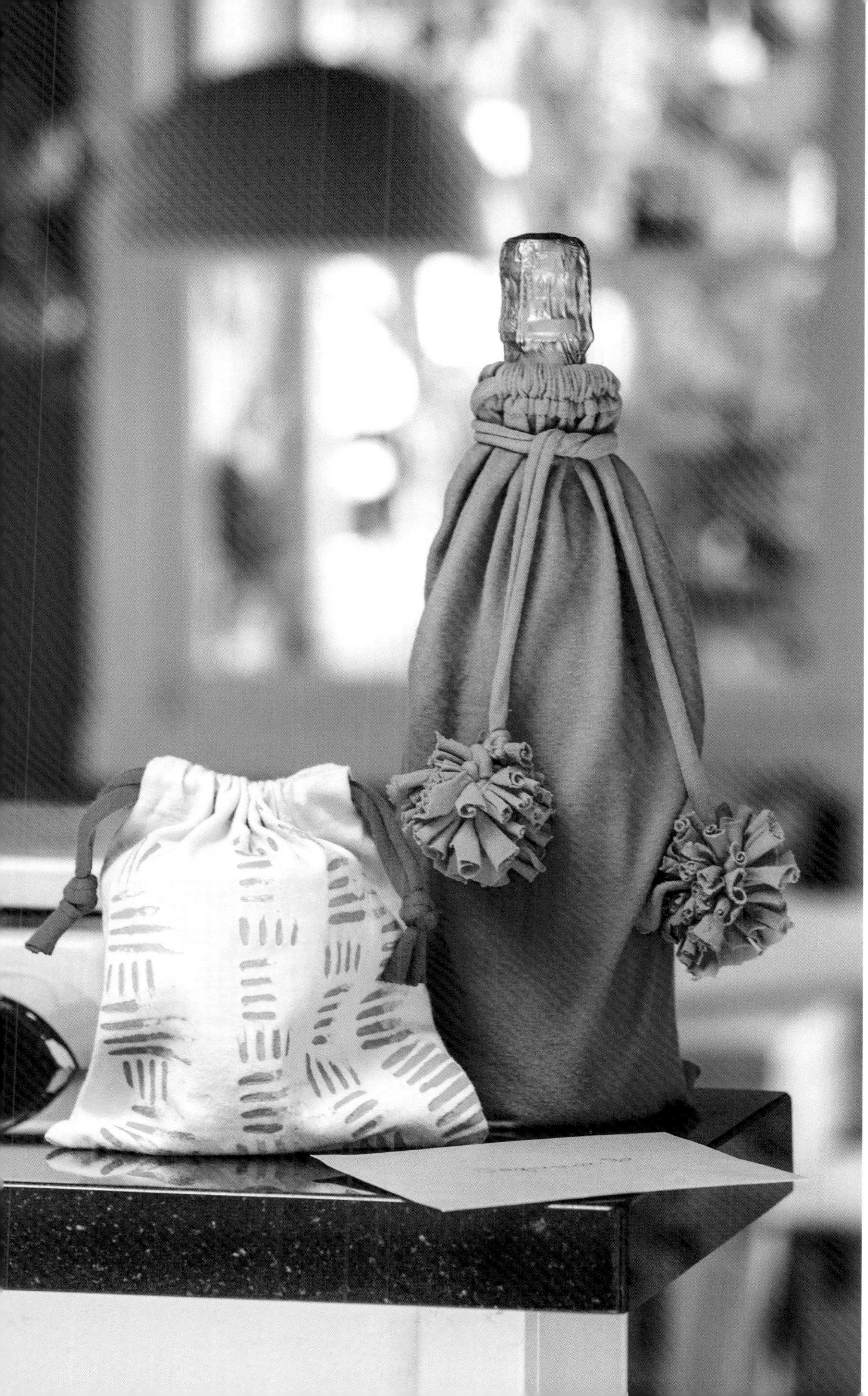

DRAWSTRING SLEEVE BAG

DRAWSTRING SLEEVE BAG *Keep things organized with these upcycled T-shirt sleeve bags. They're great when you're traveling with kids and need a place to stash some toys for the restaurant or some Cheerios for a road trip.*

Feel free to change the size of your bag to fit your needs. All you need is a longer sleeve!

➤ YOU'LL NEED

Sleeves removed from T-shirt

24″ of T-shirt yarn per bag

Needle and thread

Prep

1. Cut sleeve from T-shirt body or use scrap sleeves from previously disassembled tees.

2. Use a ruler and rotary cutter to square up the sleeve, removing the uneven shoulder edge but keeping the original sleeve hem in place. Remove all the serged seam bulk (usually at the underarm and shoulder).

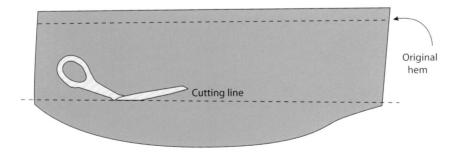

Original hem

Cutting line

3. Fold the sleeve with right sides together. Match along the edges. Feel free to pin. The original hem will be at the top.

4. Beginning just below the hemline, use the zigzag stitch to sew down the short side. Stop, with your needle position down, when you reach the bottom corner. Lift up your presser foot, and turn the bag 90°. Put the presser foot back down and continue sewing the long edge. Backstitch to secure threads.

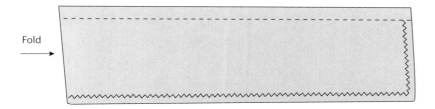

Fold

5. Snip the corners and any threads. On the folded side of the bag, make a ¼˝ cut in hemline to create an opening for the casing. Turn your bag right side out.

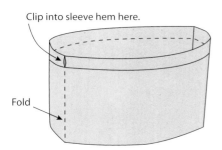

Clip into sleeve hem here.

Fold

6. Cut the length of T-shirt yarn in half. Attach a safety pin to an end of 1 piece of yarn. Using the safety pin, pull the yarn through hem opening and out the other side. Repeat this process with the second piece of yarn, pulling it through the hem on the other side of the bag. Tie the strands of yarn together with a knot at each end.

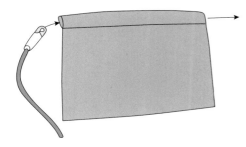

Bag to Save the Planet

If you're thinking, *It's a sleeve*, think again. Measuring approximately 5″ × 8″, a colorful Drawstring Sleeve Bag serves a variety of uses—which means that other bags don't have to be used and tossed.

- Organize game pieces.

- Keep valuable jewelry safe while traveling.

- Pack a picnic and use it for dry snacks, utensils, and to keep napkins from blowing away!

- Keep a small toy stash in your purse.

- Discreetly carry around your mama cloth or feminine products.

- Use it as a makeup bag.

- Use as a wristlet on the go.

- Keep your coupons handy.

- Hang your garden bulbs.

- Wrap gifts in it.

- Make goody grab bags.

REUSABLE PRODUCE BAGS *Why fill your reusable grocery bag with a dozen single-use plastic bags for your fresh fruits and vegetables? These lightweight, recycled T-shirt produce bags offer a sustainable and smart way to cut down on another major source of plastic bag waste and are fun to make! When asked, "Paper or plastic?" I respond, "Neither! I brought my own."*

YOU'LL NEED

T-shirt

40″ of T-shirt yarn

Safety pin

Serger (*optional*)

tip >

Gardeners! Reusable Produce Bags are perfect

for storing bulbs through the winter.

Prep

1. Lay your T-shirt on a flat surface. Measure and cut 10″ from the bottom of the T-shirt.

2. Fold in half, matching up both side seams. Measure 8″ from side seams to center. Cut vertically, so now you have 2 pieces, for 2 bags, 10″ × 8″. (If your bags end up a little bigger or smaller, that's okay!)

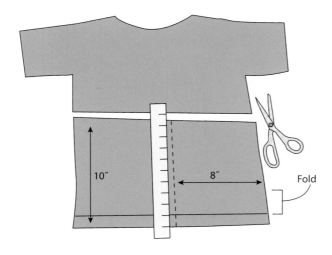

Cut the Vents

1. Unfold and refold the bag so that right sides are facing. Lay the bag onto the table with hem on bottom. Now fold the hem up 2″.

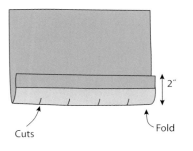

Cuts   2″   Fold

2. Using a pair of sharp scissors, make ¾″ cuts on the fold line you just created, spacing every 2″. Stop 1″ from the edge to ensure that you have room for the seam when you sew the bags together.

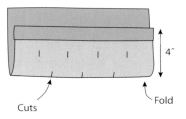

Cuts   4″   Fold

3. Fold the bottom up again, 2″. Make cuts that alternate with those (between those) in row 1. Continue until you come to the bottom edge of the bag.

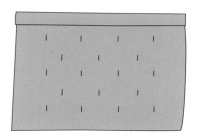

Sew

1. Pin the edge of the bag together and sew a ¼″ seam, starting along the bottom and then up the side. Then using a zigzag or stretch stitch, sew across the bottom and up the side of the bag.

2. Cut 20″ of T-shirt yarn. Attach a large safety pin on an end. Feed the safety pin through the hem casing and all the way around the bag. Tie off with a knot. Turn bags right side out.

 tip >

I use a serger when making my produce bags. If using a serger, run the stitches along the bottom edge and off the end. Cut the thread tail and then reposition the bag so that you are beginning at the bottom corner. Be sure to serge over the top of the initial stitches, up along the side edge, and veering off the bag just before you come to the hem casing. Use a yarn needle to tuck your serger tails into the seam.

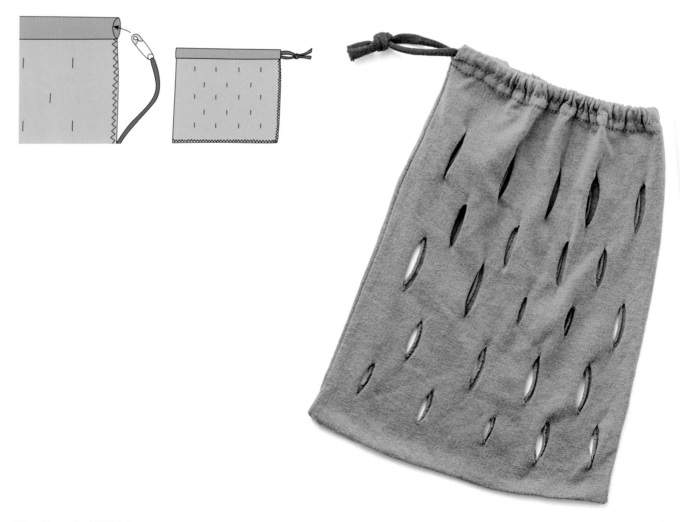

TRIANGLE MARKET BAG

TRIANGLE MARKET BAG *What can you fit inside your triangle tote? Just about anything! It's perfect for taking to the market and lightweight and compact enough to keep in your purse.*

▸ **YOU'LL NEED**
2 large T-shirts

Prep

1. Place a T-shirt flat on your cutting surface. Smooth out any creases to ensure that your cuts are even. If not, you'll find jagged edges that you will have to trim later to even up. That could alter the size of your bag.

2. Create a template from the Triangle Market Bag pattern (pullout page P2). Place the template so that it lines up with both the shoulder seam and the fold at the side of the T-shirt. Cut through both layers of the T-shirt using a rotary cutter. Keep the shoulder seams and the side folds. (I am always looking for ways to use existing seams.) This is T-shirt A.

3. Flip the pattern to create a mirror-image triangle. Then repeat Steps 1 and 2 on the second T-shirt. This is T-shirt B.

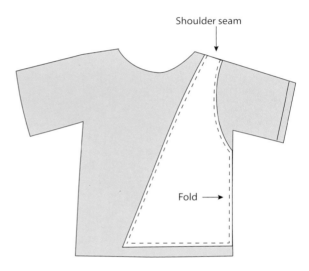

Shoulder seam

Fold ⟶

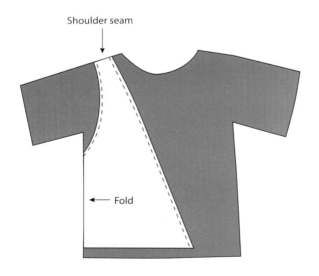

Shoulder seam

⟵ Fold

tip ⟩

I've included a pattern for a template that can be used on any large or extra large T-shirts (pullout page P2). You can make a Triangle Market Bag from any T-shirt with a few simple cuts. Use a straight edge to draw a line from the shoulder seam across and down to the bottom hem. Cut along the line. Remove sleeves. (See Deconstructing a T-Shirt, page 10.) Pin all around the finished cutout. Use this as your template to trace and cut out the same piece from your second T-shirt.

Sew

1. Open T-shirt A and lay it flat, right side down. You'll notice a subtle crease line just below the arm cutout; use that as a visual marker for center fold. If there is no crease, you can fold the piece in half and lightly press one.

Open T-shirt B and lay it on top of T-shirt A, right side down, with the edge of T-shirt B at the midpoint of T-shirt A. Match the bottom hems and pin along the bottom where 1 shirt overlaps the other.

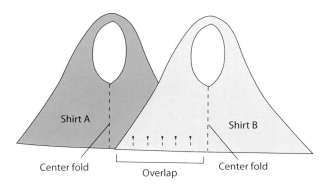

2. Fold T-shirt B in half first, and then fold T-shirt A over the top. Pin along the bottom where T-shirt A overlaps T-shirt B, through the top 2 layers of fabric.

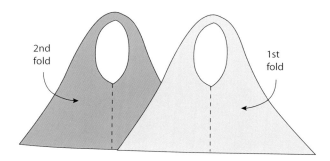

3. Now pin through the top 2 layers along the edge of T-shirt A, from the hem up to the V at the top of the overlap. Using a coordinating thread and removing the pins as you go, sew a straight line through 2 layers of T-shirt— from the V down to the bottom on 1 side of the bag. Flip to the other side and repeat the pinning and stitching on the other side of the bag.

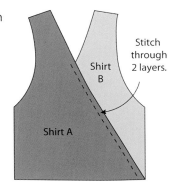

4. Turn the bag inside out and match up your bag handles (or armholes) so that they create a rainbow or arch facing you. Carefully lay the bag onto your work surface. You just shifted the bag from half T-shirt A and half T-shirt B to look more like a color-blocked V.

5. Pin the bottom hem and sew closed through all 4 layers. Then turn the bag right side out and you're ready to go shopping.

tip >

Here's my very best tip for remembering to bring your reusable bags when you go to the market: Write *Reusable Bags* at the top of every grocery list.

Resources

YouTube: search "Jenelle Montilone, arm knitting"
youtube.com

Bernina: sewing machines
berninausa.com

Pellon: Sheer-Knit Interfacing, Clear-Fuse, Peltex I Ultra Firm, fusible interfacing
pellonprojects.com

Creatiate: hand-crafted rubber stamps
etsy.com/shop/creatiate

BATTING:

Quilters Dream Batting: Dream Green
quiltersdreambatting.com

The Warm Company
warmcompany.com

WIDELY AVAILABLE:

Omnigrid Rulers

Coats & Clark threads

Styrofoam

Jacquard Products dyes

Bibliography

Rivoli, Pietra. *The Travels of a T-Shirt in the Global Economy: An Economist Examines the Markets, Power and Politics of the World Trade.* Hoboken, NJ: John Wiley & Sons, 2005.

"Municipal Solid Waste," Wastes, Non-Hazardous Waste, US EPA, U.S. Environmental Protection Agency (2012 report, updated 2/28/14), epa.gov/epawaste/nonhaz/municipal

"Textiles," Wastes, Resource Conservation, Common Wastes & Materials, US EPA, U.S. Environmental Protection Agency (updated 4/28/14), epa.gov/epawaste/conserve/materials/textiles.htm

"Textile Recycling Fact Sheet," SMART: Secondary Materials and Recycled Textiles, 2012, smartasn.org/educators-kids/textile_recycling_fact_sheet.pdf

"Cardboard Recycling Factsheet," Planet Art Environmental Foundation (updated 11/08/13), recyclingweek.planetark.org/documents/doc-152-cardboard-factsheet.pdf

"Recycling Facts," Recycle Across America, 2014, recycleacrossamerica.org/recycling-facts

About the Author

Jenelle Montilone is a recycling and repurposing revolutionary, passionate about family, the environment, and following dreams. Her love for hiking, nature, and being outdoors led her to pursue an environmental education degree in college. When she looked deep into the eyes of her firstborn, she started to wonder what types of problems his generation will face. Jenelle believed that she could make a difference, and she knows that you can too! Learn about her commitment, and join the movement to change the way we consume and create at trashn2tees.com.

Photo by Jenelle Montilone

127

stashBOOKS®

fabric arts for a handmade lifestyle

If you're craving beautiful authenticity in a time of mass-production...Stash Books is for you. Stash Books is a line of how-to books celebrating fabric arts for a handmade lifestyle. Backed by C&T Publishing's solid reputation for quality, Stash Books will inspire you with contemporary designs, clear and simple instructions, and engaging photography.

ctpub.com